D# 232410

RUNNER'S GUIDE TO CROSS COUNTRY SKIING

by Dick Mansfield

ACORN PUBLISHING

P.O. Box 7067 Syracuse, NY 13261-7067

Printed in United States of America

Library of Congress Cataloging in Publication Data

Mansfield, Dick, 1940–
    Runner's guide to cross country skiing.

    Bibliography: p.
    Includes index.
    1. Cross-country skiing. I. Title.

GV855.3.M36 1986   796.93   86-10952

ISBN 0-937921-46-7 (pbk.)

Contents

1. Getting started

Another dark November workout. Wind-driven sleet pelts your face as you run your daily route and you think, "I've got four more months of this stuff to put up with."

If you live and run in the "snow belt," November through April is a series of challenges. Short days, icy roads, and encroaching snowbanks make running difficult and dangerous. Yet, most of us still head out the door every day. Neither rain, nor snow, nor sleet .... will keep us from our appointed rounds.

But, as more and more runners are learning, there is a great alternative to slogging through the slush. Cross country skiing, one of the North America's fastest growing outdoor sports, provides the runner with an excellent complement to a year-round running program. Not only does it give one of the best cardiovascular workouts of any exercise, skiing relieves the jarring of daily running while helping to build upper body strength. And it might just make you a better runner in the spring. St. Lawrence University coach Paul Daly, who has won masters championships in cross country skiing and is an accomplished runner as well, believes, "Cross country skiing is not just an alternative, it is a way to really improve your running."

A number of runners, many from Switzerland and Scandinavia, have excelled in skiing as well as running. Ingrid Kristiansen was on the Norwegian ski team and won three silver medals in national championships before deciding to concentrate on her running. Gabriele Andersen, who has won the Great American Ski Chase series, has long been a top runner and skier. Many runners have used cross country skiing in their off-season workouts, runners including Jacqueline Gareau (who once completed the 100 mile Canadian Ski Marathon), Grete Waitz, Dick Beardsley, and Hal Higdon.

Markus Ryffel, the Swiss runner who won the Silver medal with a 13:07 5,000 meters at the 1984 Olympics, has used cross country skiing for years. In 1980, while in training in Oregon, he was unable to run due injury but could ski without pain. As a ski coach said, "His technique was ragged but he just worked hard at it. We smoothed him out and although he had never raced much on skis, he went down to California and finished fifth that year in a big 25K." Ryffel used skiing in December and January as the main part of his training and began a transition back to running in February.

Many top collegiate runners have traditionally run cross country or track and skied in the winter. Dorcas DenHartog, competing for Middlebury College, won the Division III 1985 NCAA women's 5000 meters cross country race and in 1986, finished 4th (2nd American) in the NCAA cross country skiing championships.

Runners who cross country ski shrug off the lousy running days of late fall for they know that better days are just ahead. Their "other season" is about to begin. Cross country skiing turns winter from being tolerable to being downright enjoyable.

Cairn Cross, who worked for the U.S. Ski Association (USSA), says,

Icy roads and encroaching snowbanks can make winter running difficult and dangerous.

"When I see runners out slogging through six inches of new snow, I want to stop the car, roll down the window, and ask if they've tried cross country skiing."

That's what this book will do — roll down a window to shout that there's a great winter world out there for northern runners who choose to ski. There's no need to hang up the "waffle-stompers" but there is a chance to give the legs and running shoes a few days off, by learning how to weave skiing workouts into the running schedule. Whether you have thought about cross country skiing, been out touring a few times, or even are becoming pretty competent on the slats, in the following pages you will learn about skiing from a runner's viewpoint.

WHY SKI?

The running boom of the 1970s and 1980s was launched by Frank Shorter's dramatic marathon victory at the 1972 Olympics, an event watched on television by people across the continent. A similar phenomenon took place only four years later at the 1976 Winter Olympics when a young Vermont skier, Bill Koch, surprised the world and won a silver medal, the first medal ever garnered by an American in Olympic cross country skiing competition. His success triggered an explosion in the cross country business. This growth spurt brought thousands of novice skiers into the sport. Like the running boom, the growth in nordic skiing has leveled out, yet each winter, cross country skiing gains more serious enthusiasts. Runners, bikers, canoeists, and tri-athletes use the sport for a winter training alternative. As runners of the 1980s change from quantity to quality in

Courtesy of Michigan Travel Commission

There's a great winter world out there for runners who choose to ski.

their running and look for cross training opportunities, cross country skiing presents a natural substitute. Running prepares you well for nordic skiing — it is the basic training tool of most serious skiers.

AVOID OVERUSE INJURIES

Physicians and runners agree — cross country skiing is very gentle on the legs and joints. Dr. Edward Hixson, a sports medicine authority, says, "There are fewer over-use injuries associated with skiing, the incidence is much higher with running. A runner may strike the heel with three times his body weight, where with skiing, he rarely exerts more than 1 ½ times his body weight with no where near the impact. Most runners will find that if they do have over-use problems with the lower extremities, the problems will go away when they get on snow and get skiing." Dean Anderson, a Wyoming runner, put it like this: "Minor leg problems exacerbated by constant running disappear virtually overnight when I switch to skiing in the late fall."

This relief is especially appreciated by masters runners. Ed Buckley, nationally ranked (60-65) in running, is also a medal-winning nordic skier. He says, "Skiing's a great thing for the body — you get away from all that pounding for a while. It's a real nice change."

Cross country skiing is a good change-of-pace for runners who have worked all summer and fall on the roads, perhaps finishing with a marathon. It gives one something to look forward to and helps fight off the staleness or boredom of constant running.

John Dimick, with a 2:15 Boston finish and a win in the New Orleans

Courtesy of California Office of Tourism

Cross country skiing can be "poetry for the soul."

marathon to his credit, has used cross country skiing as a training supplement. Dimick, a Vermont runner who has retired from the elite racing scene, feels that many "snow belt" runners could benefit from skiing. "Why beat yourself?" he asks. "Why not take some of the drudgery out of training? Use the winter to your advantage."

He knows whereof he speaks. Back in the late 1970s when he was competing seriously, he spent about one-third of his winter training time on cross country skis. "I came out of that year with real good strength — it took me about a month to get back into full running shape. That was the spring that I finished thirteenth at Boston."

For snowbound runners, skiing provides not only a chance to focus on a different aerobic endurance activity, it also presents a chance to be refreshed, both physically and mentally. Dick Kendall, a nationally-ranked runner in the 55-59 age group says, "For me, skiing is a change of pace. It's poetry for the soul."

And for others, skiing generates enthusiasm because it opens up a whole new world of PRs. "I've pretty well topped out in running," notes masters runner Doug Allen, a 45-49 runner with a sub-37 10K best. "I've only been competing in cross country skiing for a year but I'm setting PRs in every race. I love it."

IMPROVE OVERALL FITNESS

Cross country skiing is generally recognized as the most effective cardiovascular exercise. You can gain more aerobic conditioning from skiing because skiing involves a larger percentage of the body than running. It is able to place heavier demands on your aerobic capacity. World class cross country skiers have been compared with other international athletes and have been found to have the highest maximal oxygen uptake (VO2 max) of the group. (To review briefly, maximal oxygen uptake is simply a measure of the output of the heart multiplied by the oxygen content of the blood. As a person gets in better shape, the number of oxygen-carrying red blood cells increases.) The elite skiers were found to be the best at providing and metabolizing oxygen.

But don't conjure up a picture of an exhausted ski racer hunched over his ski poles, panting and ready to vomit. In spite of skiing's excellent aerobic workout, it's far from being a treadmill test on snow. Bob Hinman is a 54-year-old runner who just took up skiing. He completed his first ski marathon (31 miles) in a little over six hours. The next day he was up before dawn for a sunrise ski tour with his wife — in the afternoon he took a five mile run. "I can't believe how good I feel," he reported.

The demands of cross country skiing come in spurts and while you can get a good anaerobic test climbing a steep hill, you also get a welcome rest on the downhills. In fact, for a while, until you get your techniques polished, you may find it hard to get a good solid ski workout in the time you have available.That is one reason why most runners who ski still run a few days each week all winter. Not only do they keep their specific running muscles tuned up, they also get a quick efficient workout. Coaches suggest that you run short to medium distances at a moderate pace during your weekly runs. Many runner/skiers either alternate workouts or run during the week and ski during the weekend.

So, whether you want to rest injured running muscles, fight the doldrums of winter, or just maintain or improve your fitness during the cold weather months, the world of cross country skiing awaits. As a runner, you are in better shape than most beginning skiers before you even bend over to latch on a pair of skis. With some work — which turns out to be fun — you can use that good conditioning to get going and to get running on skis. Cross country ski season generally runs from January through March in most of the northern states but, in some areas, we can ski as early as November and as late as April. Obviously, a lot depends on the weather. It pays to be ready to go when the snow hits. Runners who decide to take up skiing have a few choices to make before they ever strap on skinny skis. Get these choices out of the way early so that you can get the most out of the ski season once it arrives.

BUY OR RENT?

The first decision a runner faces about skiing is: What to do about equipment. This subject will be discussed in greater detail in the next chapter but the choice basically comes down to a "buy or rent" decision. Here are some factors that a runner should consider when getting started:

1. How much money do I have to spend initially?
2. Where will I be doing my skiing?
3. How often will I be skiing?
4. How close is a reputable cross country center?
5. How easy am I to fit, size-wise?

Many articles on cross country skiing recommend that you rent equipment a few times to see whether you will like the sport enough to justify an investment in equipment. That is not a bad idea but in general, renting doesn't work for most runners. Here's why. Most of us run every day and set up routines and stick with them. The same goes for skiing — we want to get out and get exercising. If getting ready to ski turns out to be too much of a hassle, we'll simply lace up the running shoes, go out, and trudge through the slush. We're not going to drive somewhere to rent gear only to find that "all the size 9's are gone" or that there is a big crowd waiting to be fitted. So, one of the barriers to renting for runners is convenience. The other barrier to renting ski equipment concerns the quality and condition of the gear. For runners interested in performance skiing as an exercise supplement, rental equipment will not give you a true picture of what skiing is all about. Most rental equipment, while safe and adequate, is not be what you will end up skiing on. The touring skis will most likely be waxless, the boots and bindings the older-style 75mm, and the poles flimsy. It is fine equipment for beginners but it is slow, heavy gear. It's a little like going out for a run in a pair of borrowed Nike's that a friend has used to train for a couple of marathons.

Regardless of what books and articles and your friends say, do not be afraid to step right out and buy your own ski equipment. For a runner who wants to take advantage of the winter, it is a safe investment. You can find out how to buy the right ski gear in Chapter 2.

WHERE TO SKI

Just as we are free to run on a limitless variety of roads and trails, so it is with cross country skiing. For many who ski, this "getting away from it all" is what nordic skiing is all about. Unlike those who ski downhill, we are not

Courtesy of Michigan Travel Commission

The trails at touring centers can get crowded on weekends.

dependent on ski areas or ski lifts — and the costs that come with them. We can ski wherever there is snow.

Runners who plan to use skiing as a training tool will want to find a place to ski with prepared trails. In order to get a good workout on high performance skis, set tracks and groomed snow is important. Yet, you can, with experience, ski anywhere the snow is packed.

Look around for potential areas to cross country ski, places where you can set up a training route to use winter long. Ideal spots have open flat terrain with some shallow hills — municipal parks and golf courses are good possibilities. Many skiers who share areas with snowmobiles find that the machine-packed trails are pretty good places to ski, especially if you like to skate-ski.

There are hundreds of ski touring centers that have sprung up since the 1970s. Some are major complexes with hundreds of kilometers of trails, others are associated with alpine areas, but the majority are small "mom & pop" type operations. There are many advantages to skiing at a center: the trails are groomed and tracks are usually set, instruction is available, and there is often a place to come in out of the cold and warm up. Prices are very reasonable ($4 to $8 a day with economical season passes), and each year, more centers feature night skiing and snow-making facilities. The drawbacks of paying to ski, aside from having to travel to get to the site, may be crowded trails. Runners interested in training may find the tracks clogged with slow skiers, especially on weekends. But, if you pick your spot and your time, you can find plenty of room to ski. Kevin Kearney is a masters runner who is also a competitive skier. "I ski every night on a lighted loop in my town," he says. It's like having my own training site."

There are many other places to ski. State and national forests often have miles of trails available for ski touring. Some hiking trails can be skied during the winter but be cautious. Just because a ranger tacked up a "Ski Trail" sign at the trailhead doesn't mean that the trail is within the ability of a novice. The best bets are those trails that follow old logging trails or fire lanes that are unplowed. Chapter 7 will discuss ski touring in more detail.

If you can find a spot that is readily available for skiing, you will be able to pack that much more skiing into your schedule. If you have to drive a long way to find areas to ski, take heart. One of the joys about cross country skiing is that you can ski for hours at a time, take a break, and ski some more. You can pack a lot of exercise into a Saturday outing and still have energy to drive home.

WHEN TO SKI

All it takes is about six inches of snow and you can be skiing. On the first few outings of the year, carry a plastic scraper along because the ground often is not yet frozen and your ski bottoms can easily collect mud and ice. If you have new skis, be careful the first few days of skiing, it is easy to score the bottoms of your skis. Most serious skiers have an old pair of "rock" skis that they use for early training outings as well as again in the spring when they expect to tangle with rocks and dirt.

Short days and early darkness make skiing during the week a problem for those who work during the day. Some runners ski only on the weekend and run, as they have for years, during the week. Others alternate days between skiing and running. If you have a nearby ski center with lighted trails, it is a lot easier to integrate skiing into your program. Night skiing can also be done on moonlit nights or by using a miner's headlamp. Headlamps are lightweight and since they do not bounce as in running, are quite comfortable.

As a beginner, the best use of the skiing time is to work on your technique. It will take some time to become proficient. Don't plan to use skiing as a complete replacement for conditioning — use your runs to get your "aerobic fix" until your technique gets better.

When you can, try to fit a long skiing workout into your exercise program. Cross country skiing allows runners who have to squeeze in short training runs all week the chance to go out and exercise for hours at a time — without the risk of overuse injuries that long distance running causes. If you are in shape from running, it is no big deal to ski for several hours at a good pace and be ready for more skiing after lunch.

Skiing can be a great leveler of abilities — it is one sport where one can go out with the family and get in some training. Runners know how hard it is to match up with other runners, especially family and friends. If you run at a seven- minute pace, it is tough to jog very long at a 10 minute pace and the reverse is even more of a problem. Skiing allows a better chance to go as a gang. It may pay to squeeze in a short run beforehand so that the ski session is extra exercise, not a workout. Dress warmer than usual, you probably won't work as hard as when you train. If you are touring and crave more activity, break the trail for the extra exercise. Being able to ski with friends and family is cross country skiing's bonus for runners.

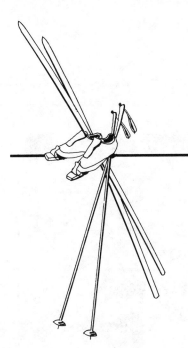

2. Gearing up

Think about your first running outfit and how it compares with your gear today. Cutoffs, grey sweats, and sneakers were part of the "start-up" gear of a lot of runners. Now, the basic equipment of most serious runners involves nylon shorts and singlets, weather-proof warmups, and several pairs of good running shoes. Many of today's skier/runners started the same way — jeans and nylon shells over long underwear and a starter set or rented ski equipment. Later, they upgraded.

If you plan to get serious about skiing and perhaps try some citizens' racing, the time will come, probably early on, when you want to buy your own equipment. If you thought selecting a pair of running shoes was difficult, wait until you face an array of skis, poles, boots, and binding systems. Here is some help on how to proceed.

WHAT TO BUY

Buying ski equipment is a lot like choosing running shoes, you tend to get what you pay for. While most of us may have difficulty noticing a difference in performance between a pair of $45 shoes and a $90 pair, with skis a doubling in price results in a marked degree of improvement. If you buy low-priced discount store skis, you very well may be disappointed by their performance. It's like trying to run in cheap sneakers — your body knows the difference.

Ski equipment can be divided into several categories. First on the rung is the economical starter package, priced for under $100, featured in virtually all ski shops and department stores. This gear, as might be expected, is low quality, quite often carryover equipment from years past, and may turn you off from skiing altogether. Many low-cost ski bases just don't perform because either the base is very slow or else the "no-wax" pattern is ineffective. The skis lack the camber needed to support active skier/runners, the poles shatter or lose tips and baskets — our attic is filled with "one-of-a-kind" leftover poles, all of varying length.

For runners who must keep to a bare bones budget, an inexpensive nordic package will get you going. But, look at this equipment as a short-term purchase — to be upgraded in a year or two, especially if you plan to do a little racing. Discount skis can be a great second pair when rocks and mud abound but you still want to do some skiing. They are also good for kids, who will outgrow cheap sets as fast as they will expensive ones. However, unless you plan to buy a pair of skis that will be used later as a second pair, or that will be handed over to offspring, think twice about the low cost gear.

Runners face a decision between training shoes and racing flats and skiers have a similar choice to make. There are three basic types of skis for runners — touring, light touring, and racing skis. (Many shops will also carry mountaineering skis and telemark skis.) Touring skis are wide, stable, and can be used for track skiing as well as "across the hills and dales" touring

Skis should be short enough to have fun on. There is a good market in "outgrown" kid's equipment.

and can also be used for racing. The next general category, light touring, fits many runners. Available in the package price range of $150 to $200, these skis will be more responsive and good for learning, touring with friends and family, or entry-level citizen racing. Light touring equipment is available in complete packages or can be set up for you by a good ski shop from a wide range of equipment.

Are you the type of runner who dives into a new sport headfirst — do you covet a Kevlar canoe for triathlons, do you want to upgrade that bike? If the answer is yes, you should think about starting right out with racing skis — just to avoid having to upgrade later on. There are some good buys in the so-called "citizens' racer" category, especially as the new skating skis flood the market. Racing skis are ultra-light, ultra- skinny, and sometimes, a bit skitterish at first for the new skier but they will give you a true taste of the fun of performance skiing. You need a packed surface to use racing skis, they are not made for tromping through the wilds. Because of this, there is a limited market for this equipment — most folks buy lower priced packages — and if you shop carefully, you can set yourself up for performance skiing for under $300.

Don't worry about those who warn that "light racing gear is impossible to handle." Many coaches feel that it is no more difficult to learn on super-light gear than on wider, touring gear. Comparing the selection with biking, it is a lot like getting on light wheels for the first time — you can't believe the responsiveness. Regardless of what equipment you start with, you'll probably end up on racing skis before long. Keep that in mind as you consider your initial selection. Don't be afraid to spend a little extra because you'll get a little extra.

WHERE TO BUY

You'll hear about real bargains at ski swaps and lawn sales but until you know what to buy, I suggest that you look elsewhere. Likewise, until you are savvy about equipment selection, steer away from the stores that promote with price, their motive is to move as much equipment as possible. In order to get their ski gear out the door, they may not be too fussy about getting the right equipment on the right person. Ski coach Roger Weston says, "Most ski shops don't keep up with what's going on. They sell skis too long and poles too short. You walk in the door and they say, 'Well, you look like a pair of 215's will fit you.' "

Seek out a reputable shop, a "specialty shop," and talk to the folks — they should be willing to take the time with you. You may have to pay a little extra for that but it's worth it to know that your skis have the right camber for you, your bindings are on to stay, and your skis are prepared properly. Do some homework on your own — talk to skiers, dig through old copies of *Cross Country Skier*, see if there is a nordic ski club in your area and talk to some of the members. (Many ski shops give nordic club members discounts of 10-15%.)

Shy away from the ski shops that carry a lot of alpine (downhill) gear - it is unlikely that they will have a good nordic department. Look for the places that sell bikes, canoes, backpacking gear and have salespersons who are skiers, preferably racers. Visit them on off-peak hours and explain your situation — that you want to ski for alternate exercise, may want to race, and don't have much money to spend. You don't have to buy the "packages" that the store will have. Ask them to select gear to arrive at what is best for you and your budget. The shop will mount the bindings and should prepare the bases so that you can walk out the door and be ready to ski.

If you are far from ski shops that carry performance gear, consider buying from one of the mail order firms. Reliable Racing in Glens Falls and The Racing Stripe in Toronto are two possibilities. Their prices are fair and their equipment selection is extensive. You will need competent assistance — latch on to a knowledgeable skier before you pick up the phone.

WHEN TO BUY

If either a friend or someone in the ski shop can help you pick equipment, buy in late summer or early fall when you can often get the best price. These will be "carryover" goods that were either held over from last season or bought at the end of last season for early promotion. Late spring is also a good time to shop for bargains. Most shops will discount ski packages but a lot depends on the time of the year — and the margin the shop got when they bought the equipment. It is just like pricing running shoes: if it's the latest high tech design such as skating skis and bindings, the ski shop probably paid top price and there will probably be little discounting. On the other hand, if the shop was able to get skis at the end of the season discounts and hold them over for a discount package in the fall, you may be able to pick up quite a deal.

WHAT ABOUT WAXING?

Runners who decide to look at light touring or entry-level racing skis will have a basic decision to make — do I buy "no-wax" or waxable skis?

Ever since their introduction in the 1970s, waxless skis have appealed to many skiers because of their "strap them on and ski" characteristics. For runners, it is as easy as lacing up a pair of running shoes.

Waxless skis, developed in the early 1970s by Trak with the introduction of the now-famous "fishscale" pattern, have been pooh-poohed by purists for years. The pattern the skis leave in the snow and the swishing sound they make during the glide has been considered the mark of a beginner. But, as in running, racers show the way for the rest of us and when Bill Koch skied a leg of his 1976 Olympic Silver Medal win on waxless skis, no-wax skis gained respectability in the U.S. and began to sell. Now, three out of every four sets of cross country skis sold in North America are waxless. The efficiency of the skis has improved as new designs are developed but there still is a tradeoff — they are not as fast as waxable skis.

Waxless skis come in many systems, each designed to provide the grip on the snow needed to push off and glide. Positive base skis have a pattern molded on the base of the ski so that the fishscale or diamond pattern (there are many variants) sticks out from the base. These skis work best on crusty and icy snow. Negative-based skis have a pattern cut into the base, somewhat like the treads on a snow tire, and are best for loose snow. Then there is a whole generation of chemical bases and "hairy bases" which have mohair-like synthetic fibers under the foot. These systems, with proper pre-treatment, are best suited for wet conditions.

Waxless skis can strike a happy medium for runners. They work well on hills but are slower on the downhills and the flats. While they don't glide as well or climb as well as a properly waxed pair of skis, they are much more efficient than a pair of skis with the wrong wax. As one runner friend of

Grip wax allows you to push off when doing the diagonal stride.

mine says, "The way I ski, I don't want to go any faster." For runners who just want to get out and go, and probably won't race, waxless skis may well be the ticket. You don't tinker with your shoes for 15 minutes, why should you with your skis? Yet, for proper performance, waxless skis will need to be cleaned frequently and have glide wax on the tips and tails. There are new sprays that you can use to improve the performance of your waxless skis in certain conditions.

Wax provides the grip on the snow needed to do the diagonal stride, the primary technique used by most skiers. When your weight is on a waxed ski, snow crystals penetrate the wax and allow you to push off with that ski — the ski literally grips the snow. As the ski moves forward, the wax releases its hold and allows the ski to glide. This "grip and glide" is the key to proper waxing.

So, to wax or not to wax, that is the question. The feeling of a correctly-waxed pair of skis can't be matched. They glide smoothly and grip the snow so that you don't slip when climbing or pushing off. Improperly-waxed skis are a pain and give you plenty of exercise — either you slip and slide or else you end up walking with half the ski trail sticking to your skis. You can waste precious time fooling around with wax, time that could be spent on the snow getting in better shape. Yet waxing is part of the mental challenge of cross country skiing to many performance-oriented skiers.

Don't let skiers hype you about how difficult waxing is. There is a certain mystique, a certain lore, that is closely tied into the psyching done on the racing circuit, however, waxing is not difficult in most snow conditions. Wax systems are color coded and easy to learn and are covered in more detail in Chapter 10. One of the best sources on how to wax skis is John

Caldwell's *The New Cross Country Ski Book,* which, packed with information, is now in its seventh edition. It should be part of your ski library. My original copy from 1971 is dog-eared and covered with klister wax from years of being toted around in wax kits.

The rapid rise in popularity of skating (Chapter 5) for performance skiing is moving serious skiers further away from no-wax skis. There is no need for a "gripzone" and, in fact, no-wax patterns drastically cut down the glide making it hard to skate. If you plan to compete in citizens' racing, you'll probably try skating. That alone may help you make a decision toward waxable skis. Waxing is becoming simplified as skating enters the picture. Gone is the need for 35 colors of wax; skaters simply glide wax the whole ski bottom and go.

BASIC SKI TERMS — LEARNING THE LANGUAGE

How do we find out what kind of running shoe to buy? Aside from reading some of the articles and the ads, have you ever gone up to a runner after a race and asked how he or she like their running shoes? I do it quite often, especially when I spot someone of my build wearing what looks like a new model. Who wants to wade through terms like curved or straight last, heel counters, poly-you-name-it shock absorbing sole? Most of us just want to cut through the "techno-speak" and find a shoe that works.

It's the same way with skis. Do we really care whether our skis are made with injection molding or torsion box construction? What we need to know is what's the best ski for our athletic ability and pocketbook. It doesn't hurt to ask a few questions. When I'm looking for skis, I ask citizens' racers how they like the racing skis they've got on, whether the skis are hard to handle, where they bought them, etc. Just like runners, skiers love to share that kind of information.

You should expect the ski store personnel to be to be able to talk about side cut, camber, and flex. If they look bewildered if you mention these terms, you'd better look elsewhere. But, in order to ask intelligent questions and make an informed choice, runners should have a understanding of some of the ski lingo. If you want to dig into technical specification of skis in more detail, several of the books listed in the Appendix will give more help. Here are the basics.

The *width* of the ski is measured in millimeters. The widest skis, touring skis, are usually 50 to 55 mm wide since they need to support your weight in untracked snow. Light touring skis, more suited for packed areas, are narrower, about 48-50 mm. Racing skis are the narrowest, often 44 mm wide.

The difference in the width of skis from tip to tail is called *sidecut.* You can easily see this by putting a pair of touring skis side by side on the floor — most likely the tips and tails will be touching but there will be a gap in the middle. That gap is the sidecut and it ranges from zero for many racing skis to 10 mm for touring skis. Sidecut make the ski turn easier because the tip and tails dig in when the ski is on edge.

For years, *length* of skis has been measured by the "arm-in- the-air" method. Many ski stores and rental shops still have you raise your arm and recommend that the tip of the ski come to your upraised wrist. Be careful. This method is pretty old-fashioned for today's skier, especially with skating becoming so popular. There is no handy formula that works — ski length depends upon not only your height but your weight and your athletic ability. (A heavier skier may use a slightly longer ski than a lightweight; a better skier often will use slightly longer skis.) Most men use skis that are 205 to 215 centimeters long while those who skate use shorter skis (190 to 200 cm.) Many women ski on 180 to 195 cm skis. Don't buy skis that are too long, shorter skis are easier to handle.

Camber is the arch of the ski that holds the patterned bottom or "grip wax" off the snow when you glide. *Flexibility* is what allows the ski to bend to grip the snow when you put your weight on it and push off. Flexible skis are called soft-cambered skis while stiffer skies are called, just that, stiff skis. In order to get proper performance out of your skis, the camber must match your weight and leg strength. If you have too soft a ski, you'll drag the middle section during the diagonal stride and cut into your glide — if your skis are too stiff, you'll slip and slide all day.

There are several ways to select the proper camber. The easiest is to squeeze the skis together. If you can do it with one hand, you've got a pair of soft-cambered skis. Now try to squeeze a pair of racing skis together — you will probably find it impossible to completely close the gap between them. These skis have what is called "double camber," one camber but with a stiffer section in the middle. Most runners will find that they will opt for light touring skis, which can usually be squeezed together with both hands. The squeeze comparison, is just that, a comparison between skis, not an absolute test.

Although some ski shops class it in the same category as the "raise-an-arm" system for ski length, the "paper test" still can be used to help select skis. First, find an uncarpeted level floor, lay the skis on the floor and place a piece of paper under the skis at the point where the bindings go (the balance point). Then stand on the skis and have the salesperson or a friend move the paper. There should be a slight drag on the paper. If you've pinned the paper to the floor, the skies are too limber which means you'll end up dragging the ski and getting more training than you bargained for. Conversely, if the ski is too far off the floor, your kick zone will never make enough contact with the snow and you will slip.

Calibrated camber testers are used by some ski shops to match skis to skiers. These gauges measure the force it takes to close a pair of skis, sort of a mechanical squeeze test. The reading is then, using a chart for weight, matched up with a skier. These systems are used mostly for racing skis although most racers agree that because of each person's weight and leg power differences, the best way to select skis is to go out and ski on them. Good ski shops will help you with the decision. They may even have a pair of "loaners" of different widths and cambers that you can try out before making the final selection.

Skating skis often have softer camber, allowing a constant pressure to be applied along the whole ski. They may have imbedded steel edges as well as multiple grooves. Camber becomes of little concern if you plan to skate since you will be using the side of the ski, not the grip wax, for propulsion.

It is easy to get mired in the technical aspects of ski selection. Most recreational skiers and citizens' racers could care less if their skis have side cut or whether they have soft tips or stiff torsional flex. We want skis that will be comfortable, long-lasting, and will help us go for some age group awards. In spite of the "techno-speak," it is just like buying running shoes.

BOOTS AND BINDINGS

Cross country boots parallel the ski categories There are touring, light touring, and racing models. (You also can buy boots suited for mountaineering or telemark skiing.) Runners will generally lean toward the light touring or racing models whether or not they plan to race. These boots are lighter and much more like running shoes in design and feel. They also are a lot warmer to wear than the earlier models.

Touring boots are usually made of leather and have the widest sole of the group and a 75 mm toe. This Nordic Norm boot design, along with the 3-pin "rat trap" bindings that fit it, are still the most popular design in the United States. If you rent skis, this is the system you'll likely be handed. These inexpensive boots and bindings have served millions of skiers well for years and are practical for the more rugged touring treks. They are a little heavy for track skiing although many good skiers, including citizens' racers, find that these old favorites fit the bill. If you want to minimize your investment, this is the way to go. There is a wide array of 75 mm used gear available.

The light touring and racing systems are newer arrivals to the nordic scene. Featuring a 50 mm toe, they have less drag for track skiing. The touring models are cut higher while the racing boots are very similar to running shoes. Manufacturers of these systems have gone their separate ways, so in many cases, unlike the 75 mm bindings which are essentially generic, the 50 mm bindings are not compatible. Be sure to match your boots to your binding system.

Ski boots are sized using the European system so you will have to do some experimenting to get a correct size. Wear several pairs of socks when

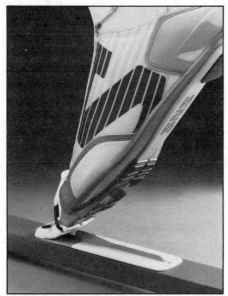

A new generation of ski boots and integrated bindings has been designed for skating.

trying on boots. Many runners use a light polypropylene sock and a white woolen running sock for most conditions. The boots should fit snugly with some room in the toe — if they're too tight your circulation can be cut off resulting in cold feet; if the boots are loose, you run the risk of developing blisters. If you have trouble with width or length, try another brand. Boots from different countries sometimes have slightly different characteristics.

A new generation of ski boots has been designed to be used for ski skating. These boots, and their integrated binding systems, provide the lateral stability needed to skate effectively. Take a serious look at the skating boots if you are planning to citizens' race.

Runners interested in racing may opt for racing boots and a multi-purpose light touring ski, with plans to pick up racing skis later on. Conversely, some skiers use light touring boots on racing skis. Pick a system that is comfortable, you'll most likely be using them for a while. Ski boots, unlike running shoes, don't wear out very fast — I skied in one pair for ten years.

POLES

Over a quarter of the thrust developed by an accomplished cross country skier comes from the ski poles. Runners realize this at once when, after skiing, they feel the tenderness in the triceps and other upper body muscles. It pays to have a pair of poles that will be a help, not an energy drainer.

Until recently, most of the ski poles that came with ski packages were bamboo (tonkin cane). These have been replaced by low-cost fiberglass poles which are stronger and more durable.

Runners who purchase light touring gear or who become interested in performance skiing will want to consider stiffer, stronger poles. These are made of stiff aluminum or carbon fiber and sell for $25 to $50 a pair. Serious racers get into more exotic materials like Kevlar and graphite for the shafts of their poles.

You will see a lot of different baskets on poles. The traditional circular baskets are good for skiing in unpacked snow or for general touring. Skiers who frequent areas with groomed trails will want to look at the light half-basket poles. These, because the basket doesn't bounce the tip out of the snow, are more efficient because the tip stays in the snow better during the end of the poling thrust. Racers use a variety of streamlined baskets, all of which are unsuited for general touring. While you are looking at baskets, notice the tips of the poles. They will be curved backwards which helps with the withdrawal of the pole from the snow.

For any but the cheapest ski poles, there will be a right pole and a left one. The straps give the clue. The top strap should be on the outside of your hand. (Mark your pole handles so that you don't have to figure out which is which when the wind is howling and you want to get exercising.) Poles should have a knob at the end and the straps should be adjustable.

Learn how to put on the pole straps in the warmth of the ski shop. Bring your hand up through the loop of the strap and then grab the handle — you should feel the strap snug against your hand. As we will note in Chapter 4, the straps help you develop power during poling and, properly adjusted, allow you to rest your hands during the backswing. (That's what the knob is for, it should rest easily between your thumb and forefinger as the poles are extended backwards at the end of the poling stroke.)

What length should your poles be? The standard method to determine pole length has been to have them come up to your armpits as you stand on a hard surface. For runners planning to compete, a slightly longer pair help develop more power. Runners who plan to skate should use poles that are at least chin high, and probably nose high. (See Chapter 5)

Buy stiff light poles of adequate height. Poles that flex are inefficient — some of your energy is lost in the bending. Poles are easy to upgrade because they are relatively inexpensive. For your first purchase, think about getting good general purpose touring poles with round baskets. Then, as you ski, try out other types of poles of varying lengths. Later on, you can then make a better choice of racing/light touring poles and still have your old poles for family outings, backwoods tours, or training runs.

CLOTHING

If you are a winter runner, you already own about everything you need to get out cross-country skiing. You are also aware of some of the dangers of winter running/skiing, the effect of wind chill, and the need to especially protect the extremities. If you are male, you also know the need for crotch protection in the winter. Wind chill becomes even more of a factor in skiing because of the speed you attain on the downhill runs.

Skiing in a wind-proof warmup suit over polypropylene underwear and a turtleneck does the trick in most skiing weather. It's a loose outfit, one that you probably already run in, and if you get too warm, you can tie the jacket about your waist. Use what you have — if it works for running, it will be fine for skiing.

Courtesy of Oregon Department of Transportation

Dress in layers and dress for what you will be doing. If you are out for a tour with friends, dress as you would for a winter walk. On the other hand, if you are going racing, you can, just as in road racing, get by with a lighter outfit because of the body heat generated. Use the lessons you've learned from running — it is easy to shed extra clothes. I carry a garbage bag folded up in my fanny pack for emergency clothing and a pair of socks which can also double as extra mittens.

You will find that due to the poling action, your hands will most likely stay warmer than they do in running. Consider buying some cross country ski gloves which will help your poling. Shy away from the super-thin racing gloves — it is easier to deal with sweaty hands than cold ones. Err on the side of warmth.

Knickers, knee socks, and a light parka used to be "in vogue" as the perfect cross country outfit. While these are still fine for the tour, many track skiers and most racers are choosing the new form-fitting one piece outfits. There are not many options. Either you wear your running gear, or knickers, or one of the Lycra-style suits. Many runners who get into biking face the same dilemma, you really don't want to appear to be a "middle-aged flash" in a hot Lycra suit. On the other hand, the outfits are not only functional, they are comfortable. One piece skiing suits are great for citizens' racing but if you are on a tour, wear warmups or extra layers. The suits cool down fast as soon as you stop exercising.

The main trick to "gearing up" to ski is to first decide on a pair of skis of the right size and camber, pick a pair of poles of the right length and stiffness, and the rest is old news. We fit ski boots just as we do running shoes and can use most of our running gear as is.

Skiing gives runners many things to add to the Christmas or Hanukkah wish list (Santa brought me a one-piece racing suit not long ago.) You will want a fanny pack for lugging extra clothes and snacks. A headlamp will allow you to go out skiing in the evening. Let's see, a waxing iron, a pair of polypropylene gloves, a pair of gaiters (to keep the deep snow out of your boots), and oh yes, Santa, a pair of ski stockings.

Runners can outfit themselves with used gear from a "ski swap" for under $100 or can spend five to ten times that amount getting ready to go. In any case, get to know your specialty shop folks; they can be invaluable in steering you toward ski gear that will get you off and running — on skis.

Headlamps are lightweight and easy to use for night skiing.

3. Training for cross country skiing

Swedish ski coach Kjell Kratz is one of the most successful nordic coaches in the world. His skiers swept the Worldloppet marathon series from 1983 to 1985. In a ski clinic in the United States, he noted that many American coaches and skiers feel that bicycling is better training for cross country skiing than running. Kratz doesn't agree. He believes that a solid running program, using hills and trails, is a better training method.

Cross country skiing has a lot in common with running. A runner who has been running all season can start out on X-C skis right after the first snowfall and ski comfortably. Many do. The first few ski outings often brings out some tenderness in some unused muscles, especially in the upper body. Some runners who plan to ski will integrate some minor changes into their fall running program before they hit the ski trails. With just a little extra effort, others train more specifically for cross country skiing.

As runners, we know it is easy to get obsessed with piling up mileage. It can be comforting to be able to say, "Yes, I averaged 65 miles a week for the ten weeks before the marathon." But, just as runners have learned to get away from accumulating "junk miles" in their training, skiers likewise aim for quality in training. For most, there is only a limited amount of time available for workouts. Inclement winter weather and early darkness make it tough to find time to squeeze skiing workouts into the work week. "Canned" training formulas don't fit most people. Most of us need to find out what works for our situation — to aim for a combination of running and ski-specific workouts to use before the season and then, after snow arrives, a system of on-snow and off-snow training that will work throughout the winter.

TRAINING WITH THE BRAIN

In military flight training, student pilots are continually judged on an item called "headwork." Headwork is how one uses common sense before, during, and after a flight. It is a term well-suited for physical training as well — how we use our head may well determine how effectively we train, how well we use the limited time available to us, and how much fun we have while training.

Many articles have been written about the problems of overtraining and many of us have been participants in the "mileage mania" that has characterized the running boom. One writer put it like this, "At times it appears to me that the medal winners in our major competitions are not necessarily the most talented runners, but rather those with adequate talent who have survived their training programs." When we take up a new sport, be it biking, triathloning, or cross country skiing, it is easy to fall prey to overtraining when, with our enthusiasm for the new activity, we neglect to back off from our running. Instead of being complementary, the new sport places added stress on joints and muscles.

John Underwood is a former steeplechaser who, after studying exercise physiology in Finland, traded his running shoes in for ski boots. Having seen the way that the Scandinavians train for cross country skiing, he is convinced that North Americans tend to work too hard at training. "We train too hard, too close to the anaerobic threshold," he says, noting that anaerobic activity generates lactic acid at a rate faster than the body can handle it. "We don't do enough easy training. The Finnish skiers train from April to November on building an aerobic base. Only when they get on snow do they work on developing specific muscles." Underwood compares aerobic training as the building up of an aerobic reservoir which is then drawn upon as skiers race throughout the season. It is not unlike the training program that many running coaches espouse for running quality races — build the aerobic base and only then, add some hill work, intervals, or Fartlek. If we have not raced too often or trained too hard, runners arrive at the start of the skiing season with a good aerobic reservoir.

Aerobic training goes by many names: base training, endurance training, or distance training. Regardless of what it is called, exercise physiologists and coaches suggest that runners and skiers do most of their training in the aerobic zone. In order to stay in the aerobic zone, you first need to estimate your maximum heart rate. Women should subtract their age from 220; men should take ½ their age and subtract it from 205. The aerobic zone is about 60% to 80% of this figure. Exercising below this range has, in the eyes of many experts, little training value. Exceeding it, which is easy to do in sprints, on hills, or during races, actually can detract from the aerobic base.

It is difficult, even for well-coached athletes, to train aerobically, to back off and stay in the aerobic zone while training. Prompted by the Seiko on the wrist, it is tempting to push just a bit harder, to beat the last training run time by a few seconds. Since we are using the total body in skiing, it is easy to overdo it. As one ski coach put it, "We need kinesthetic cues to reading our various limits, the kind of thing that runners have traditionally done by trial and error." One way to do it is to learn what breathing patterns correspond to a particular heart rate. Anaerobic threshold, for example, is about the point where you are breathing hard but not gasping for breath.

Another monitoring method is to take your pulse during and after a workout. As you probably know from running, it is not always easy to do. It is even more difficult with ski poles and gloves to contend with. A better way is to use a heart rate monitor. More and more athletes, even "weekend warriors" who work out for fun and to keep the weight down, have used heart rate monitors. Now in a price range that is affordable by more runners and skiers, the devices are easy to use.

The first time I skied with a heart rate monitor, I learned fast how to pace my workout. It was something I had not thought too much about before that. The beeper on my wrist was set for 140 and sure enough, on every hill the thing began to beep. (Quietly, I might add — we don't need to advertise the fact that we are overdoing it.) As I began to relax and think about how to keep in the training zone, I did better. A quick pause here, a little shift in skiing cadence there, and I found that I was using my head.

What sort of a training program do we use? A friend of mine, planning to open a fitness center, promised that if I would join his club, that he would guarantee to take minutes off my 10K time. Then, with a smile, he said, "Of course, first thing you've got to quit your job."

So it is with so many of the training programs written up for runners or skiers. Designed by the elite runner/skier, they assume that we have plenty of time, perfect weather, and a fat checkbook. "Cookbook" training programs simply do not work for most runner/skiers — we've got too much else cooking in our lives.

So the trick is to train aerobically, to tailor a personal workout program and weave some ski-related activities into our roadwork. This chapter will cover some training equipment and routines that can get you ready for cross country skiing. Fortunately, the easiest way to train for skiing is to do just what we've been doing — by running.

TRAIN TO SKI BY RUNNING

The quadriceps, "quads" as the bikers say, are the muscles in the front of the upper part of the leg and are important to cross country skiing. You can work on these muscles by running hilly terrain. Serious skiers, like serious runners, run hills. Many coaches recommend that their skiers use leaping, bounding strides up the hill to imitate the diagonal stride movement. For ski-skating, skiers bound more off the inner leg muscles and don't run directly up the hill but rather run from side to side as they climb.

If you already run hill repeats, keep at it in the fall. For most runner/skiers, just running a rolling course on soft ground will be more suitable than intervals and repeats. Another good way to condition your legs for skiing is to run cross country in the fall. Run some of the same trails where you will later ski to get a sense of the terrain. If you like to compete, find a couple of cross country meets in your area — they will give you plenty of hills.

One caution — be aware of hunting seasons — they start very early in many parts of the country. Runners in upstate New York and Vermont, my training locales, have to contend with bow-wielding deer hunters and bird hunters in early October. Think about adding a new aerobic routine to your fall runs — talk or yell, or even sing, as you run in the woods. I'd rather be considered a little whacko than be mistaken for game. Wear your fluorescent vest and red clothing. (I have a red wool cap and bright orange cloth gloves that do double duty as the days get colder.) Do not wear white, it can easily be mistaken for a deer's tail moving through the woods. Once regular season opens for deer, avoid the wooded trails altogether.

RUNNING WITH SKI POLES

Cross country skiing uses the upper body — that is one reason it is such a great workout. In order to get ready to ski, it pays to incorporate some strength techniques to your running. One way to do this is to run with weights, using a system like Heavy-Hands. A much better way is to run with a pair of ski poles — it not only helps build strength, it gets you used to the rhythm of skiing.

Hank Lange, a fine triathlete and former U.S. Ski Team coach says, "Runners can get off the roads and run with poles in the woods. The varying terrain is a nice break. I run with my poles up hills or sometimes I just hike. It not only gives you a whole new perspective on your running, it also benefits both your running and your skiing."

Find an old set of poles of the right height (just a little shorter, 5-10 cm, than you'll ski with) — I use a bamboo set that are held together with duct tape. You can pick up a used pair at a rental shop or ski/skate exchange or

Try running some of the trails you'll ski later on.

check with skiers in your area. Many families have collections of old poles that came with "starter sets" that have been out-grown or up-graded. Slide or cut the baskets off to avoid entanglements in the woods.

Unless you live in the middle of ski country, you may feel a bit foolish at first, clacking down the road with a pair of ski poles. ("What's she up to now?" you imagine your neighbors saying.) Start off on trails and woods roads if you can, even the local schoolgrounds, so that you can have a private spot to get started. The softer terrain is easier on your arms and legs.

The trick to training with poles is to run naturally and just gently plant the pole when it is ready, about every other stride. I find that my ski pole comes down about every two strides — in other words, my right pole strikes once for every two strikes of my right foot. If it doesn't work out quite like that, it is no big deal, the idea is to let your arms swing normally, just like you will do when you ski. You will find that it is more tiring than straight running, even though the ski poles are light. Run your normal routes at your normal pace, or at first, even a little slower. Try not to concentrate on the poles, just let them come down naturally. After a few tries, your self-consciousness will vanish.

Most skiers concentrate on the hills when using poles; some practice bounding up the hill, simulating the push off of the diagonal stride. Others work on the staggered double pole used in skating, planting their poles just as in skiing. When running with poles, try to lift yourself up the hill with each pole plant, using your arms to help propel you up the hill. The feeling will be very much like the thrust you'll get from your poles while skiing.

Aside for getting your upper body in shape, you'll get some side benefits — nasty dogs who harass you all year find other things to do when you run by carrying ski poles. Poles also help your balance and traction when the leaves underfoot are wet or when the first slushy snows come. By the time skiable snow arrives, your ski poles will feel like old friends, and your arms and shoulders will be ready to tackle the hills in earnest.

BIKING FOR RUNNERS/SKIERS

If you have brought bicycling into your training regime, you've gotten a good start to X-C training. Some elite skiers, having suffered more injuries from running in the off-season than they do from skiing, have made biking their preferred spring/summer aerobic workout. Nowadays, biking is increasing even more in popularity with nordic skiers because, being an exercise that builds the quads, it is quite specific training for ski skating. The pace of biking — the work on the uphills and the recovery on the downhills — is also similar to skiing. Most coaches recommend that biking be used to get in the long distances needed to build a good aerobic base, rather than hammering the legs for long distances.

Mountain bikes, the 18-gear go-anywhere bikes that have become so popular, can fit right into the training program of many skiers. Much more durable that racing bikes, they can be used virtually anywhere and anytime. The hard climbs and thrilling descents give the summer rider a taste of cross country skiing.

Runners can also get a good workout on a wind trainer or stationery bicycle. You can read a book, watch television, or listen to classical music on a headset. But, for many, the boredom of inside biking is intolerable. Personally, I'd rather slog through the slush or ski in the teeth of a gale than

Courtesy of Reliable Racing Supply, Inc.

If you buy roller skis, get a pair that can be used for skating.

feel like a gerbil on a treadmill. But, biking, especially in the running season, is a viable option for many runners. It will help relieve their legs and joints during the running season and at the same time, help ready them for cross country skiing.

ROLLER SKIS/TRAINING SKATES

Ever crested a hill in your car and encountered a skier wobbling toward you on roller skis? You see it more and more in ski country. Buying and using a roller skis or training skates is a serious commitment toward skiing. If you shell out over $100 for a pair, you may have made the transition from a runner who skis to a skier who runs. It happens every year to many runners, watch out!

Roller skis have been used by serious skiers for years. They are an excellent training device, the closest thing to actual skiing, but can also be a good way to maim yourself. Most longer roller skis, designed for diagonal stride and double poling, are sitting around unused these days as most racers are skating. These older rollers have a ratchet arrangement that allows you to push off for the diagonal stride. Skiers use them for diagonal stride on the uphills and for double poling on the flats. Some enterprising skiers are cutting them short so that they can be used to practice skating.

If you are going to purchase roller equipment, buy a system that allows you to skate. The newer generation of roller skis is short, without ratchets or brakes, designed for skating. They cost $175 to $225.

The Rollerblade® training skates, used by speed skaters and hockey players as well, are the choice of many competitive skiers. Prices range from $100 to $135.

Courtesy of NorthAmerican Sports Training Corp.

Training skates are a favorite training method of the Canadian Ski Team.

You can use your regular ski poles for roller skiing but must replace the basket and the tip with a unit designed for the roads. Roller ferrules cost about $10 and have a hard carbide tip better suited for asphalt.

Speaking of which, just in case you meet asphalt "up close and personal," wear long clothing when you try roller skiing. Knee pads and a bike helmet might save your hide. If you can, stay off the roads altogether at first. Use a high school, factory, or church parking lot. Go there during off-hours to practice. Once you are comfortable, find some hills to practice on. Do not roller ski downhill — there's no training gained and the risks of injury are obvious. It is safer and more beneficial to take off the skis and jog down, then ski back up.

If you get into roller skiing, work with a coach or a knowledgeable skier. You can pick up some bad habits in both the diagonal stride and in skating using rollers. (You'll tend to push off too late in diagonal and skate on the edge of your ski in V-skating.)

Roller ski races are a good summer workout and one more type of competition for those so inclined. Some races use a mass start while others use an interval start like a bike time trial. Roller skis vary greatly in speed — some roll much easier than others. It gives those of us who are back in the back of the pack a new excuse — "Darn rollers were slow."

STRENGTH TRAINING

Cross country skiers carry more weight than runners, in fact, some good ones look more like wrestlers than marathoners. That solid, powerful look comes from a strong upper body, something most runners lack. Much of the power in skiing comes from poling. Runners may want to do some specific training to get the upper body ready. The best exercises are those that simulate the movements of skiing. That is why running hills with ski poles is so beneficial.

ARM STRENGTHENERS — Back before hi-tech exercise devices were touted in glossy mail-order catalogs and inflight magazines, nordic skiers were nailing old bicycle tubes to trees or posts and, standing as they would on skis, training by yanking away. (Coach John Caldwell and his crew of national ski team members from southern Vermont pioneered the use of the inexpensive training aids in the late 1960s. In the lore of cross country skiing, these tubes are known as "Putney arm bands.") While bike tubes or elastic bands certainly still work to simulate poling motion, there are several devices on the market that are lightweight and portable. Exer-Genie and Excel's 10/190 exerciser are two that can simulate diagonal poling technique.

ROLLERBOARDS — Another homemade training device, first used by the East Germans, is the rollerboard. It has been part of many a serious skier's workout routine since the mid-1970s. It consists of an inclined plywood ramp, a dolly with castered wheels, and a pair of ropes. You lie or kneel on the dolly and pull yourself up the incline with the ropes. A good description of how to make a roller board is in Bob Woodward's book, *Cross-Country Ski Conditioning.* With a couple of sheets of plywood, some 2 X 4's, and some wheels, rope, and fasteners, you're in business.

WEIGHT TRAINING — You don't need weights to do weight training — the roller board is a good example. Coach Hank Lange thinks that you should move your body instead of moving weights or pulleys. He suggest that you perform repetitions quickly, simulating the action you are going to perform. Pullups, situps, pushups, and roller board are the weight routine of many a good skier.

Nautilus and Universal machines are excellent for conditioning runners for skiing. Nearly all stations are helpful, in fact most coaches suggest that you use them all and not get too specific. Runners will find that the Super Pullover machine is especially helpful for poling and the abductor/adductor machines good for the skating muscles. Free weights, especially with low weights and high repetitions, are useful in building upper body strength. Get some coaching unless you are already competent in lifting.

Strength training should be done on easy days. If you run every day, take a run first and take it at an easy pace. Walk in and take a break before hitting the weights. Strength training should be done two or three times a week at the most.

NORDIC SIMULATORS — Pick up nearly any magazine and chances are you will see an ad for a nordic simulator. The two that are cited as being most specific to cross country skiing are Nordic Track and Fitness Master. Both of these offer "jar-less" aerobic exercise and are generally considered to be effective for conditioning. The devices have their detractors and their supporters. Because either is a significant investment, it pays to check them out closely beforehand. Some fitness clubs have these machines along with Nautilus and Universal equipment. If you have barbells or an exercise bike gathering dust in the cellar, think twice before investing. Neither machine is especially applicable if you plan to ski skate.

GETTING IN SHAPE TO RACE

Runners can train for skiing during ski race season by continuing to run during the week and training on skis whenever possible. For most runners, this means most skiing is done on the weekend. Some skiing should be done at race pace to get used to skiing at a sustainable race pace. It will take some time to get a sense of what works — remember that it didn't come right away on the roads either. As we learn to race, we need to get a sense of just how fast we can go 15K. One of the best, and obvious ways, to do this is to simply go out and race a few times — the more you race, the better sense of pace you will have. Then you can work even more effectively on your skiing.

I have a couple of courses that I ski and, just like running season, I keep track of my time for each workout. Yet, times will vary: some snow is simply faster than other snow. It is best to measure your pace by how you feel — and train toward the side of taking it a little easier. As runners, we are not used to the overall effort of using arms and legs and it is easy to get carried away a bit if you don't monitor your exertion. The "talk test" works just as well for cross country skiing as running, especially for the longer training sessions.

Canadian national ski coaches Jack Sasseville and Anton Scheier, writing in *The National Guide To Loppet Skiing*, say, "Make your easy days easy enough so you can go hard on your hard days and make your hard days hard enough so you have to go easy on your easy days." Got it?

We can learn to ski faster by being more relaxed and efficient. Canadian coaches like to say, "Quick and light." U.S. coach Roger Weston yells to his skiers as they skate up a hill, "Take time to relax. Make it feel like a dance. That's the way, looking good!" And he adds sotto vocce, "It's easier to say than do."

RUNNING DURING THE WINTER

"Specificity" is a term that we hear frequently when reading about cross-training or triathlons. There is a "use it or lose it" element to training that will cause most runners, even if they get serious about skiing, to continue their running all winter long.

Noted orthopedic surgeon Stan James, who excels in running and skiing at the Masters level, believes that "while cross country skiing in the winter will provide great cardiovascular fitness and great total body strength for the runner, the primary training mode must be running."

Hal Higdon, another great Masters runner who loves to ski, is also a believer in specific training. He says, "If you want to run better, you run. It's that simple."

Have fun at winter road races but take it easy if you've been doing a lot of skiing.

Most experts believe that you should run at least once or twice a week during the winter. If you run several times each week, make it a moderate workout. Forget speed work or very long distance. You will find that skiing has your lungs and upper body raring to go but your legs will have lost some of their running strength. I notice it after about five miles or so — the knees feel a little tight and the calf muscles get tired.

Former U.S. Nordic coach Mike Gallagher put it like this in a *New England Running* article: "Runners have to maintain contact with their running. Otherwise, you lose your running rhythms and running coordination, not to mention the loss of strength and fitness in specific muscle groups which don't exactly apply to skiing."

One good way to put some zing into your running workouts is to enter a couple of winter races — the "frostbite specials" or Super Bowl fun runs that are low key and frequented by the gung-ho of the running community. Just take it easy, remember that your running muscles are on a winter break. Winter relay races, where you can either run or ski — or if you are brave, skate or snowshoe, are quite widespread. If you are inclined toward triathlons, there are a growing number featuring running, skiing, and snowshoes.

The great thing about cross country skiing is that it is an alternative, not an addition, to running. It allows you to back off and let the legs heal, the toenails grow back, but still keep in good aerobic shape and maintain your weight. Don't defeat the purpose by overdoing it on the roads. Once or twice a week is fine. If you are getting itchy, back off the skiing and ease back into the running. Find the balance that fits your body and the winter conditions around you.

4. Up and running on skis

Cross country skiing can be a paradox to aerobically-fit runners who, having read about what a total cardiovascular workout skiing is, give it a try and then have a hard time getting their heart rate into the exercise zone. While quite easy at the basic recreational level, cross country skiing takes some practice and technique to get the kind of workout one gets from running. Yet it doesn't take long to get proficient. Here's how to get started and how to get better.

Runners are, in most part, self-taught and self-coached. We read articles on training, talk to friends, and then just go out and run. Sometimes it takes advice from others to change our style of running. I learned that several years ago, at the end of a hilly 10-miler in Vermont, when one of the early finishers was walking back along the route to encourage finishers. "Pump your arms more, Dick," he yelled as I passed. He told me later that I was running with virtually no arm movement — at least when I was tired. It took another set of eyes to spot that — and his comments gave me something to work on. Even now, when I'm getting tired in a race, I think, "Work your arms," and it helps. It helps even more in cross country skiing.

In skiing, technique is much more important than in running. It pays to get some coaching early in the game. It is not just a matter of 'looking good,' it is more a matter of getting the most out of your effort. Without good technique, the good aerobic conditioning that you bring from running is wasted. Once you develop your skiing skill, you magnify your enjoyment of skiing. But beware, skiing can be addictive. More than a few runners now look at cross country skiing as being a lot more than something to do when they can't run — instead, they now run in order to get in shape to ski.

One of the reasons that cross country skiing grew so rapidly in the 1970s was the dictum, "If you can walk, you can ski." It sold a lot of skis and got a lot of people skiing — at a walking pace. Runners want a higher level of activity comparable to that of their running ability. If you jog, you'll undoubtedly want to move at a similar pace on skis while if you are a "front of the pack" speedster, you'll want to move on out on your skis as well. In either case, it won't happen overnight but it won't take too long. Skiing for conditioned runners is not difficult.

Should you take ski lessons? Each runner has to answer that question but let's look at some things to consider. Most runners can get by for a while on the fact that they have a "good motor." They can make up for a lot of inefficiency with their endurance base. One runner told me, "When I first started racing, I just went out and puffed and panted with the rest of them — it worked ok for a while."

But let's face it, there is only so much time available to ski — weekends and an occasional evening will be it for most runners. If you have to drive to find snow and then rent skis, your best bet may be to jump right into a lesson. On the other hand, if you live in the snow belt and can, like me, literally go out the back door and ski, just go out and do that. Use your

Group lessons are an inexpensive way to learn the basics.

aerobic base to gain as much experience as possible and play catch up with your technique. Pick up some lessons later on.

Growing up in Vermont, I learned to ski on my own as a kid. Like many citizens' racing skiers, I had never had a formal ski lesson and was sort of proud of it. Only recently did I learn the value of ski lessons. Not long ago, on a whim, I took my first lesson and learned that I should have done it years before.

Whether you take lessons at the start or wait until later, find an instructor who races. The person should be competent in all skiing techniques, especially skating. Look for the lapel shield worn by members of the Professional Ski Instructors Association (PSIA). Ask for a fully certified instructor and explain that you are a runner, that you'll back for more lessons if things work out. You will find that instructors, since they normally have to spend a lot of time with out-of-condition beginners, will be eager to work with motivated runners. Look for coaches or ski clubs who use video equipment in teaching — it is an effective way to see what you are doing wrong, and right.

STRAIGHT AND LEVEL
Diagonal Stride

Whether you teach yourself or go out with an instructor, one of the first techniques that you will work on is the diagonal stride. This is the traditional technique of cross country skiing and fortunately, is just like running. It is the classic image of the cross country skier, pole planted, gliding with the rear ski in the air. But, first of all, don't worry about looking like the men and women in the glossy racing photos — forget about the rear ski coming way off the track. That's the look of a highly trained athlete with excellent balance — we have a ways to go yet.

Conjure up an image of how you might run on a day when the roads are covered with wet leaves or when there's a little freezing rain glazing the streets. Remember how carefully you planted each foot and got the weight shifted on to it? That pressing down feeling is what skiers call the "kick." It took me years (teaching yourself is not always efficient) to realize that the term "kick" really was mislabled. You will use that "slippery road" push for the diagonal stride. It is a good image to keep in mind as we head on out.

Start on a level area. If you have a track to ski in, fine, otherwise just make some by walking with your skis in a straight line. Let your arms swing just as you do when walking. Turn around by just moving the tips, one at a time, like the hands of a clock, back to the reverse direction. Don't worry about your poles, just move your arms normally, keeping the poles pointed slightly backwards. Walk normally and once you are comfortable, try a little jog or shuffle, leaning forward just a bit, like we do when running.

With the example of running on a "slippery road" in mind, try jogging a little on the skis. Push off with one foot and extend your other foot. Shift your weight to the forward foot and glide on the ski that you have your weight on. This glide is the key to the diagonal stride. Don't worry if yours is almost non-existent, it takes some getting used to. With your weight on the gliding ski, push down a little more with that foot (this is the racer's kick) and bring the other ski ahead. When you press the ski to the snow, the camber of the ski is flattened out, allowing the wax or pattern on the bottom of the ski to do its thing — giving you the "grip" to push off. Keep the strides short at first. Get a little rhythm going, alternately pushing and

Courtesy Salomon/North America Inc.

Let your arms swing in the diagonal stride, just as in running.

gliding. It is a lot like running on skis — with a short pause for a glide.

The diagonal stride feels unusual at first because there is no "oomph" to it like in running. When you bring your foot forward you don't get that satisfying clump of a waffle-tread on asphalt. In this case it is more like landing on a moving ski. You don't lift the foot, you slide it, so it just doesn't seem like as much of a workout.

Many runners just getting started in skiing tend to be impatient, taking shorter, choppier strides then experienced skiers. The problem is balance. Gliding along on one ski is tricky at first. We tend to bring up the other ski too soon, thus cutting off the glide. Try to extend your glide — ski instructors call it "making a commitment to the ski." Swing your arms just as when you run and your poles should flow naturally.

Every so often, you may lose the rhythm, getting out of "synch" with your skis. Most likely you are hanging back with your weight behind the lead ski. This sometimes gives the slapping sound of the ski coming down hard on the track. If this is the case, try practicing the diagonal stride on a slight uphill section of track — this will slow you down and help get your weight shifted to the forward ski. As your balance improves, you'll get up over the front ski more and smooth things out.

There are several techniques that can help you perfect the diagonal technique — one is to ski without poles. You may feel a little unsteady but concentrate on swinging your arms, just like a fast walk, and get the rhythm down. Don't forget to push off and to transfer your weight to the gliding ski, and then shoot the opposite ski ahead as you press down again. Exaggerate the arm swing and see how easy it is to get moving right along. As you swing your arms faster, your speed will increase.

Another trick that ski instructors use is to have you ski on one ski; yes that's *one* ski. You push off with your boot sort of like riding an old scooter. This exercise helps your balance on one ski which is essential in the glide. This is a good way for runners to learn to get out over the gliding ski and not be in a hurry to jog along in a shuffling manner.

As soon as you can, start using the ski poles for more than balance. Notice that as you stride on skis, your arms act just as they do in running — your right arm comes forward as your left foot comes forward. Hold your poles with the tips pointed backwards a bit (you can't get any power from poles that are straight up and down) and as your arm comes forward, set the pole tip in the snow and give a little push. If you've been running some with ski poles this should be already quite natural. Keep your elbows bent, plant the pole in the snow, and push as you drive past it with the other ski. Don't think about it too much, just be natural and let the poles come forward with your arm.

Relax the death grip on the grips, it just tires the hands. Put the weight against the straps as you push and as the pole goes behind you and your arm extends backwards, try to loosen the grip on the pole even more, until it's just between your thumb and forefinger. Experienced skiers release the grip on their poles altogether on the backswing.

Now that you have progressed from a basic jog/shuffle to a smooth diagonal stride with a rhythmic press-glide and your poling is coming along, it's time to hum the theme from "Chariots of Fire" and think about smooth and efficient skiers. Recall the last time you saw a world-class runner on television, someone like Steve Jones at the Chicago Marathon? As he clicked off sub-five minute miles, you may have noticed that his head didn't bob, his stride was straight down the road, there was no wasted effort. That efficiency, folks, is what we are looking for on skis. We all ski with our own idiosyncrasies, but we want to try to go smoothly down the track, all our efforts directly ahead, without a lot of extra motion. If you enter a 50K marathon later on, these little improvements in technique will make a world of difference in your efficiency and performance.

Double Poling

Double poling is a technique you will use a lot, especially on slight downhills where you get going a little too fast for striding or when you want a little change of pace. It is an efficient technique for beginners as well as elite racers and is simply a matter of pushing off with both poles at once and gliding along, then doing it again. You will probably find the technique tiring until your upper body gets in shape.

Start on a level area which either has tracks set or that is packed down. Begin by lining up your skis parallel, then bend forward slightly, reach ahead with the pole tips angled backwards a bit and push off with both arms. Keep the arms bent and lean toward the poles as you push. (Actually, you will be pulling against the straps, then pushing as you move between the poles.) Use your whole upper body: the trunk muscles, then the shoulders, finally the arms. Continue to push your arms backwards and you'll end up with your body bent forward, arms outstreched backwards. If everything worked, you'll be gliding forward. Reach forward and do it again. Do not end up in an exaggerated "leaning over" position as you complete the poling even though you may see racers do it.

The faster you pole, the quicker you'll go. Watch other skiers — ad-

Use the whole upper body — the trunk, the shoulders, and the arms during the double pole.

vanced racers get a lot of power out of the double pole technique. While the technique requires less effort than the diagonal stride or skating, many runners find it pretty tiring at first. Now you know why cross country skiers have trained on roller skis — it's to build the upper body muscles.

The "kick double pole" or the "one step, double pole" version of the technique brings the legs into play. This variation is used a lot by skiers on flat areas and on shallow downhills — times when you aren't going quite fast enough to use regular double poling. You may want to wait until you get comfortable with diagonal stride to work on this technique for it incorporates the same push used in diagonal. Push off with one ski and then plant the poles and double pole as the rear ski comes forward. The sequence is: stride, double pole, stride, double pole. Watch someone demonstrate it and give it a try. The foot that "kicks" or pushes off should be a little ahead of the other foot during the glide. Push or kick back just as your arms are starting to swing forward. Remember to get out over your poles with your body, using your body weight to help with the poling. (Finally, a use for that weight!) The timing gets some getting used to, but for the runner, since we use the legs in the process, it is not as tiring as the straight double pole.

Before getting too much further into how to ski, it won't hurt to think about how to fall — and how to get up. All skiers fall, even the best, so it helps to think about it a little before it happens. Falling down has sometimes been associated with failure in skiing — visions of snow-covered beginners make for a good laugh with the "apres-ski crowd." For runners, while we are not used to falling, we soon learn that it is an integral part of of learning to ski well. Learn to fall properly and look at falling and getting back up as a bonus in exercise.

Smart skiers learn to fall properly.

Knowing how to fall is important — be loose and sit down if you feel yourself going. The more you ski, the less concerned you will be about falling — it is no big deal so don't let it be. Get up, brush off, and get going. But getting up can be tricky at first.

If you are on a hill, swing your skis so that both are pointed across the hill (neither uphill or downhill). You may have to lay on your back and swing your skis over you. Now, scrunch up and get on your knees. Next, without laughing, push yourself up with your hands, pushing on the skis. Your poles may be more of a problem then a help; if so, take them off before you start righting yourself. Take your time. If things are a little tangled, take off one ski and get up, then hitch the ski back up. Friends are a big help — an outstretched hand saves a lot of effort when you are flat on your back and getting silly at your predicamant.

Most runners will be able to get a decent diagonal stride and double pole going the first time out and before long, feel pretty comfortable on the flats. But the real fun in skiing lies over in yonder hills and dales. Now that we know how to get over there and get up from a fall, we're ready for hill work.

CLIMBS

It is interesting to watch new cross country skiers deal with hills. Runners tend to want to stay on the flats where their diagonal stride and double poling has become polished and they can use their conditioning to good advantage. On the other hand, skiers with alpine experience can't wait to get up the hill so that they can bomb down the other side. Hills add an element of anticipation and rush of adrenalin that runners don't often get — except when a German shepherd makes a run at the flanks. Once you learn to handle hills, you can put your aerobic fitness to work on the climb side and get a nice rest on the downhill side. Instead of pounding down the hill on tired legs, you can grab a breather and glide down the slope. But first you need to get up to the top.

Find an easy slope with a flat area on the top and a long runout area at the bottom. The diagonal stride can be used to climb many gradual slopes. In racing, it is called "running the hill." Just as in a road race, gear down to shorter strides before the hill gets steeper. Don't stall, keep the momentum up. "Bound" more, using more weight shift, so that the patterned bottom or waxed section of the ski can grip the snow firmly. Use the poles aggressively to help you, again making more frequent pushes to match the stride. Hills are where runners find out what they've got for upper body strength after a season of running. If the skis start to slip a bit due to the steepness, you will want to shift into the primary climbing technique, the herringbone.

Herringbone

Ever seen the "crow's feet" tracks up the side of a snowy hill? That's the mark of the herringbone. On steeper slopes, skiers get more grip by spreading the ski tips apart and keeping the tails together, forming the letter "V". (No, not a "W".) Bringing the knees together slightly, roll the skis so that the inside edges dig into the snow. That gives the grip. Continue to stride as before — now you can walk or jog up the hill with the ski tips spread. Bring the poles back a bit so that you don't get tangled with your outstretched skis. Keep the pole handles in close to your body because you get more strength that way.

Courtesy of Tug Hill Tourathon, Inc.

The herringbone is used on steeper hills. Note that the lead skier has transitioned back to diagonal stride.

On easy hills, you normally will climb using the diagonal and shift to a slight herringbone as you feel your skis start to slip. The steeper the hill, the more open the tips must become and the more you need to dig those edges in. You'll notice good skiers hop up steep hills in a herringbone, jogging from ski to ski. Racers will take it the next step and skate their way right up the hill.

The herringbone is a good workout — you can easily go into oxygen debt as you climb rapidly. As in running, keep your body forward and low to the ground and look up the hill. Shorten up the strides and try to keep your momentum up. You will use herringbone a lot: for touring, especially if you get into untracked terrain, and to conquer the steep hills you'll find on many citizens' racing courses. You haven't lived until you reach the mid-point of a race, are the tenth skier in a line, all chugging up the hill with the herringbone, when the first skier falls and blocks the route. You spread your tips even wider, plant your poles, and stand there and pant. That's the herringbone.

DESCENTS

Downhills put the spice in cross country skiing. Those skinny fiberglass skis you've got strapped on can really move. Downhill skiing in cross country makes doing hill work, climbing up and skiing back down, an exciting form of exercise, not an exercise in drudgery as running hills can be. With a little work on technique, you can keep the "excitement" under control.

Now that you have climbed a gentle slope with the herringbone, try going back down. First time down, start with your feet a little further apart than what you used for double poling or diagonal. With your knees flexed, push off with both poles. Keep your hands forward a bit with the poles angled backward and bend forward slightly. Stay loose and enjoy the ride.

Try a few downhills, bending your knees to ride over the bumps. If you've watched experienced skiers, you probably noted how they use their flexed knees as "shock absorbers" to handle the dips and bumps and how they come more erect on the smoother portions of the hill. Try to keep from bending too far forward with your fanny in the air — you're pretty unstable in that position and if not careful, may get to know your ski tips "up close and personal." You don't have to ski straight down the hill. Try skiing traversely across the hill, keeping most of your weight on the downhill ski. That's how you'll handle some of the steep slopes later on.

This is a good time to practice falling. Smart skiers learn to sit down under control, sometimes called "bailing out," before they lose it altogether. Try it a few times, putting down your hands first and sitting down, then leaning off to the side. Remember to keep your skis across the hill as you get back up and use your poles to hold you until you get your skis headed back down the hill. Don't start again until you are loose and ready to go.

Downhill running on skis is why we climbed that hill in the first place — it's a good chance to catch our breath and enjoy the countryside. As you become more confident, you will want to get into a tuck position to minimize drag. But, before the countryside starts to go by too fast, it's time to learn some techniques to slow down.

Snowplow

You'll see many innovative ways of slowing down. We just discussed the "sitting down" method and you've probably also already used "drag both poles." For panic stops, some skiers use the "grab a tree" technique. For most runners getting into skiing, the best way to maintain control of the downhill speed will be the good old snowplow.

Known among alpine skiers as the wedge, the snowplow is basically the opposite of the herringbone, an inverted "V". With knees bent slightly, you push your heels out to bring the ski tips nearly together and the tails spread outward, rolling the skis so that the inner edges dig into the snow. Try it on a shallow hill, pushing out with the heels, coming nearly to a halt and then, relaxing the pressure, continue downhill. Just as in the herringbone, the steeper the hill, the wider the "V" you make with the skis. If you put more pressure on one ski, what happens? You turned slightly, right? You just learned the snowplow turn.

TURNS
Snowplow Turn

Now that you have done a snowplow turn, let's work on it. Use your hands and ski poles to help "steer" into the turn, twisting the body slightly in the direction you want to go. Use the inner edge of the outside ski to dig in. Feel the pressure need to turn? Back off on the pressure and you're right back in the basic snowplow.

Try one to the left. Push out with the right heel, keeping your hands in front of you, and shift your weight on to that right ski. Your weight is on the ski carving the turn. Practice turning left, then right down the hill.

Step Turn

At slow speeds, changing direction using a step turn is easy — it's the same way we turn when walking or running. The first trick is to start with the inside ski, that's the ski on the side to which you are turning.

Try a turn to the right. Lift the right ski tip slightly and set it down a bit further to the right. Shift your weight to that ski and bring the left ski tip up and over to match it. Make small incremental changes. Practice on the flat as you work on your double poling and diagonal stride — at the end of the straightaway, turn around using a series of step turns. (You will see folks using a kick turn to reverse direction when stopped — save that for a little later. Then, have someone show you one, it is easier than it looks.)

The step turn can be use in a number of turning situations. It is especially good on traverses across a hill where it is used to control speed. As you ski diagonally across the slope, you step up the slope a bit to slow down or if feeling brave, do a little step turn downward to pick up speed.

Skate Turn

There are times when a step turn, or even a quick series of them, won't get the job done. To negotiate the sharp curve up ahead, you may need a step turn with a little more power, you may need a skate turn. (We will cover skating on skis in detail in the next chapter.)

First of all, you need a little speed to do the turn. Think about doing a step turn with a little power behind it. First, push off the inside edge of your outside ski. Try a right turn. Instead of stepping off on the right ski, "skate" off the weighted left ski and then step with the right ski. The rest of the turn is essentially the same as you transfer the weight to the right ski and bring the other ski up to match it. Try a few turns on a shallow slope, you'll find that it is a neat way to turn.

Skate turns are frequently used by racers.

Advanced Turns

Runners are not known for caring too much about stylistic skiing. There are, however, some maneuvers that will make you a better skier on the downhills. Advanced versions of the snowplow turn are called the stem turn or the stem christie. These turns start with a half snowplow with the outside ski in the snowplow. Then, bearing down with the inside edge, you bring the inside ski parallel to the outside snowplow ski. Get an instructor to show these to you. You may want to try a few alpine lessons to get the technique down a little better.

If you haven't already, you'll soon hear about the cross country telemark enthusiasts. Ever watched ski jumpers land, knees flexed, one ski ahead of the other? That is the telemark position. Telemark turns have been around for ages but have enjoyed a resurgence of interest in the 1980s. These graceful sweeping turns that work best with steel-edged skis and powder snow are popular with skiers with an alpine background. Most runners, mainly interested in using cross country as an aerobic supplement, will tend to stick with the conventional turning techniques. Numerous articles and several books are available on telemark. If you herringbone up the mountain, perhaps you deserve to make graceful sweeps on the downhill. But, if you ride the lift up with your special skis, you probably aren't a runner.

We have looked at how to ski on the straight and level, how to climb, descend, and turn. These basics, coupled with your runner's endurance base, will allow you to ski on prepared trails, in citizens' races, or in two feet of untracked snow in the wilds of Minnesota.

5. Skating on skis

A TECHNIQUE FOR ALL

There is a revolution underway in cross country skiing. The sport is being overhauled as traditional techniques are being forced aside by a new kid on the block — skating. This makes it an exciting time to join the sport. Performance-oriented skiers across the world, looking for more speed, have changed their skiing ways and have done it over the groans of traditionalists who feel that skating will ruin the sport.

The revolution was triggered by the "Johnny Appleseed" of U.S. nordic skiing, Bill Koch, who picked up the technique in 1980 from Finnish racers. Koch skated his way to four World Cup tour victories in 1982 and went on that year to become the first U.S. skier to win the World Cup. His accomplishments sent racers scrambling to learn the technique and changed the racing scene forever. Now, thousands of skiers, from preschool children to octogenarians, are skating on skis, and loving it.

Skating stirred up a hornets' nest of controversy in the international racing community. The cool reception was a lot like that once reserved for fiberglass and waxless skis. Opponents, many of them Scandinavian, fought to restrict skating in spite of the fact that all top performers were using it whenever possible. The International Ski Federation (FIS), never known as a bastion of progressive thinking, imposed restrictions in the mid-1980s that barred skating from some races and limited it to portions of others. Helicopters were even used in some European races to patrol against unauthorized skating.

The V skate, the same skating movement that is used when learning to ice skate, is the technique that sent cross country traditionalists up the proverbial wall during the mid-1980s. Considered by some to be "ugly to look at" or even "ruining the sport," V-skating, also called vertical skating, was embraced by ski racers worldwide because it was faster than the diagonal stride. This was proven not only in calibrated tests but in hundreds of ski races. "Free technique", as skating was called, was becoming much like swimming — whatever technique got you there the fastest was the one the racers used.

To newcomers from the road racing community, the whole hassle, which continued through the 1986 season, reminded them of the earlier controversies about women running marathons. (Recall Katherine Switzer being ejected from the 1976 Boston Marathon by Jock Semple.) But, think of what would happen if a top runner like Craig Virgin introduced a new way of running — perhaps at a varied pace — the first mile at 5:00, the second at 5:30, the third at 5:00, and went on to win every road race he entered. You know that about every runner in the country would at least try a varied pace to see if it worked. That is what happened in cross country skiing as more and more skiers learned to skate and found that they could go faster. Skating is sweeping the sport, in spite of the foot-dragging (pardon the pun) of the traditionalists.

Courtesy of Salomon/North America Inc.

You can pick up a lot of skating tricks by skiing behind good skiers.

Hal Higdon, one of the best master's road runners in the world, also wins awards in cross country ski races. He says, "Skating is here, and for all practical purposes the diagonal stride is as dead as high jumping facing the bar."

Many other performance-minded runners who have taken up skiing have found that skating is not only faster, it is also a more efficient way to ski. Jim Schoonmaker, a runner turned skier, agrees, "The handwriting is on the wall. If you what to race, you've got to learn to skate."

Is skating just for racers? Definitely not. Runners who want to ski for an aerobic workout will find that ski-skating is a welcome addition to their "bag of tricks."

Runners, who come to cross country skiing without the baggage of years of diagonal stride experience, pick up skating with ease. Learning the new technique also can help perfect the diagonal stride. In the last chapter, we noted that runners have the tendency to cut off their glide in the diagonal stride, bringing their trailing ski forward too soon. The resulting "shuffle-stride" can be corrected by learning to skate. "You have to make a full commitment to the ski," explains Cairn Cross, who corrected a weight shift problem in his own skiing by practicing the skate. "By learning to glide on the skating ski, runners can really improve their diagonal stride as well."

Whether we race or not, there are several other practical reasons for runners to learn to skate. Many of us like to lace up the shoes, do a few quick stretches, and get out the door on a run — time doesn't permit much fancier preparation. It is convenient to ski the same way, snow conditions permitting, by heading out as frequently as possible, hitting the golf courses, school grounds, woods roads — wherever we can find a place to ski.

Skating allows us to do that. You can skate, if you are careful, with just a couple inches of snow. (There is no grip wax to pick up dirt and dried grass.) Skating works well on snowmobile trails, packed woods roads, many of the places we ski without groomed prepared trails. Your chances of finding a place to skate are usually better than finding a place with set tracks to diagonal stride.

You are also freed from the uncertainties of snow and temperature conditions. This is important in changing weather conditions when wax or patterned bottoms just don't work. Skating, since it does not rely on wax, allows the runner a chance to get a good workout in virtually all snow conditions. (When there is new snow and temperatures are very cold, below 0° C, skating is inefficient due to poor glide, so runners may want to use the diagonal stride technique.)

Skating is evolving rapidly. New skating techniques are being invented by enterprising racers and coaches as this book is being written (Spring 1986). Some basic techniques have been developed but there will be more. Do not let the terminology throw you — the names of the techniques are very confusing, even to experienced coaches. We will review the diagonal skate, the one-skate, the double-pole V skate, the offset or staggered V-skate, and the marathon skate. But before getting tongue-tied, let's just learn to skate.

GETTING STARTED

If there is one key to skating, it is the knack of getting comfortable while balancing on one ski. Diagonal stride requires the same ability, so it is no surprise that good skiers can do both techniques with ease. On the other hand (or foot!), beginners have enough trouble at first with the balance on two skis. It takes practice to relax and be able to glide on one ski, but that is what skating is all about. First we need a pair of skis that will glide.

The "no-wax" bottoms that work so well for diagonal stride make skating more work. The same goes for grip-waxed skis. As you transfer your weight to the skating ski, the grip surface wants to grip the snow so the glide is reduced. If you ski on waxables, scrape off the grip wax and melt some glider wax on to the kick zone. You can not get a good sense of skating when you attempt it on no-wax or grip-waxed skis. Learn to skate on glide-waxed skis.

An instructor will probably have you begin by skating down a shallow hill, without poles. This is an excellent way to learn to shift your weight to the gliding ski, to get comfortable with committing yourself to one ski at a time. To start, push off with one ski and extend the knee and hip of the skating leg. This should be a thrusting action that gets your upper body out over the leg. As you glide on a flat ski, the hips should be forward and your chin should be right over the gliding leg. As the glide ends, thrust out the other knee and transfer your weight to that ski. It helps to have the recovery leg, the ski that will skate next, brought in close to your body.

Take some time and just work on shifting weight from ski to ski as you work down the hill. The tendency is to cut off the glide by bringing the other ski to the snow, just like in the diagonal stride. Fight the tendency, be patient and work on gliding on one ski. Try lifting one ski and skiing as long as possible, then doing the same with the other foot, to help work on balance.

Once you feel comfortable going down shallow slopes, try the same on the flats. Now is the time to really work on keeping the skating ski flat on the snow. Don't cut with the edge since it will reduce your glide. Thrust your leg out with energy and get the knee out over the ski. When you are in the glide, imagine that you have a crease in your ski pants. You should be able to look right down the crease from the knee to the ski. Once you can move on the flats, it is time to pick up the poles. But, as you wade through the variations of poling techniques, remember the lessons you have learned — leg drive and balance are the key to good skating. Poling adds the extra power so that you can really fly.

DIAGONAL V-SKATE

The easiest kind of skating to learn is the single-pole V- skate. This is a skating herringbone or skating diagonal stride movement with the poles being used just as in those two traditional techniques. It is the skating step to use when you are tired in the upper body or if you are tackling a steep uphill section.

To get started, use a level spot with packed snow but without set tracks. Begin a herringbone, angling the right ski out and placing your weight on it. Then, lifting the left ski, thrust out diagonally, shifting your weight to that ski. It is just like the skate practiced without poles except now, you should help push yourself on to the skating ski with your opposite pole. Make a definite weight transfer to the skating ski and as the glide slows, pole and skate off with the opposite ski. Concentrate on keeping the gliding ski flat on the snow. Get a coach or friend to show you the correct technique — it is easy to learn.

The key is to have the skating ski moving before you set it on the snow and as you pole on the opposite side, make a complete weight shift to it. Keep your body forward and be patient — balance on the gliding ski before you use it to push off.

The single-pole skate is handy for climbs where the terrain is too steep to use double-pole techniques. You can easily switch to a herringbone if you run out of steam. For many runners who skate, the diagonal skate will be the technique that they find easiest, the technique they fall back on when they are tired.

POLING EVERY SKATE (ONE-SKATE)

Racers use the "one-skate," poling with both poles on each skating thrust, on the flats when they are building speed and on gradual uphills. This technique is fast and balances the skating action from side to side. It requires good balance and a definite weight shift. Some elite skiers pole twice or more for each skate when they are accelerating. The poling is sharp and the abdominal muscles are used — there is no time to bend out over the poles. This is a technique that is tiring for most skiers and few runners will use it for any long period of time, but it is the way elite skiers win races.

To give it a try, begin on a gentle downhill and with hands forward, poles angled back, push off with the poles. You should feel that you are pushing yourself on to your gliding ski. Get the weight out on the skating ski, just as in any skating maneuver, and then, push off on to the other ski. The tempo can get hectic on downhills if you are impatient. Watch a good skier — the glide is long and relaxed and the poling seems effortless. For most runners, this technique will be useful for practicing balance but will be too demanding to use for any long periods. We will shift to the "bread and butter" technique, the Double-Pole V-Skate.

DOUBLE-POLE V-SKATE

Watch a top level ski race and you'll see elite racers literally flying along the course, skating right up the hills. The technique that provides the power and speed is the double-pole V-skate. Start off with a double-pole. Just as the poles are planted, push off on your right foot so that your weight is on your left foot. Then push off with that foot (the left one) and transfer your weight to your right foot, then double pole and push off again. Pole only off one side (called the strong side) and then only skate off the weak side. You'll find that you do develop a lot more power off the strong side because of the double pole.

The skis should move just like in the single-pole technique — only the poling is different. Power off the inside edges of your skis as the glide ends and lean forward, using your body weight in the double poling. Before long, once you get the rhythm down, you should be able to move easily on the flat.

If you don't make a full commitment to the ski you are gliding on, it is easy to lose momentum and get hung up, straddling your skis. If things get a little uncoordinated, switch to a single-pole skate for a while, then try another series of double-pole skates. It is tiring for the upper body at first but fun once you master it.

Tall poles and staggered poling characterize off-set skating — the technique favored by most racers.

STAGGERED DOUBLE-POLE (OFFSET)

Staggered poling is just a bit more complicated than straight double-poling. It allows a more continuous period of poling and helps maintain uphill momentum. Also called offset, the technique is used by racers on the steeper sections where they can not double-pole with each skate. Offset has become the predominant skating method for most serious racers. It takes the powerful double-pole technique and adds a new wrinkle — the pole plant on the weak side is slightly delayed.

It goes like this: Assume that the right leg is the dominant one, the so-called skating leg. As you thrust out the left knee, you pole on the right side, again pushing yourself on to the skating ski. The left pole is planted shortly afterward, just as the left ski hits the snow. You should hear the stagger in the poles as they hit, sort of a "thunk, thunk" with the stagger becoming more pronounced on the steeper sections.

If you watch elite skiers cruising on the flats, you may see them skate three or four times without poling, just to rest their arms. They use the skating techniques like gears in a race car: they cruise (overdrive) with a one-skate, poling every skate. They use a double-pole V-skate (third gear) on the easier uphills, shifting to an offset or staggered poling method (second gear) on the steep sections. Only when the going is very steep, do they use first gear, diagonal V-skate. (We runners still have four-wheel drive, the herringbone, to keep us going up.) As the hill is topped, the sequence reverses. Don't get hung up on the many variations of poling — remember, the primary power still comes from the legs.

MARATHON SKATE

This is the technique that started the skating revolution. Pauli Sittonen, a Finnish marathon skier, has been attributed with the development of the marathon skate although years ago, Scandinavian hunters traveled great distances, using a shorter ski to push off with. Some runners, trying the marathon skate with today's even-length skis, will sympathize with those hunters — the technique is awkward and unbalanced compared to most skating maneuvers.

Marathon skating is used when skiing in prepared tracks. One ski glides in the track while the other is used, in a skating motion, to provide the propulsion. The technique works well when the course is too narrow to V-skate or when the skier does not wish to mangle pre-set tracks by skating across them.

Marathon skating, in spite of its awkwardness, is one of the fastest ways to travel on skis. Newer skating methods have evolved and marathon skating was cast aside for a while but it has regained popularity for use in certain situations. "It's effective in cold weather," explains Kevin Jones of Cross Country Canada. "The ski in the track warms slightly and glides better."

Runners will welcome a change of pace after V-skating, a chance to get into a set of tracks and double-pole or marathon skate for a while. The muscles used are just different enough to provide a welcome relief. Even top skiers will shift into a marathon skate — it is less demanding than other forms of skating and useful for longer tours and races. Marathon skating is a good tool in the runner's skiing bag of techniques.

The key to marathon skating is to use a powerful double pole technique.

The skating ski should stay even with the ski in the track.

It helps to get out over the poles and let the body weight provide part of the momentum. To begin, use a prepared set of tracks and a level area and get a good glide going with the double pole. Plan to skate off the right ski and leave the left ski in the track. Here comes the awkward part. After a good double pole, lean to the right a bit and lift the right ski up slightly, angling the tip outward. (Your feet should still be close together and the tails of the skis will probably be crossed.) Put the angled ski on the snow and keeping your knees together as before, transfer your weight to the angled right ski. Don't be shy about committing to the skating ski — glide on it. (Some instructors recommend that you lift the "in-track" ski slightly to make sure your weight is transferred.) As the glide ends, push off with the inner edge of the right ski and shift your weight back to the left ski which should be gliding down the track. Double pole and try it again.

Watch to make sure that your skating ski stays even with the ski in the track — if you let it lag behind, you have very little leverage to provide the push that, along with poling, is the key to marathon skating. The sequence for marathon skating goes like this: Double pole, glide on skating ski, push off, glide on "in-track" ski, double pole.

The marathon skate is a fine technique for runners interested in performance. It allows skating on many narrow courses where the tracks are set and, for some, requires less energy than the V-skate methods. Awkward at first, the technique, once mastered, can get you flying down the track.

EQUIPMENT FOR SKATING

A rash of new skating skis and skating boots has hit the cross country market as manufacturers scramble to catch up with the equipment needs of these new methods. Skating skis often have blunt tips, imbedded metal edges, multiple grooves and innovative flex patterns. Integrated boot/binding systems have been developed specifically for skating. Yet, in spite of these new high-priced outfits, the jury is still out on what the ultimate designs will be. The technology is still evolving and there is a good chance that some of the highly-touted gear may not quite fit the bill once it gets some hard use. Most of the skating skis are single-purpose and unsuited, due to the lack of any wax pocket, for anything but skating. If you plan to skate as part of your training regime, think twice before rushing out to buy the latest hi-tech system. On the other hand, any good light touring or racing ski can be used for skating and some excellent bargains are available as skating skis arrive in quantity. If you buy a dual-purpose pair of skis, keep them short.

To skate, use a shorter ski (a 190 cm or 200 cm ski if you would normally ski on a 215 cm pair) as well as a boot with a stiff sole. Longer poles work better for skating — most racers use nose-high poles. Mike Moffett is a top-ranked racer from New York state. "Last year," he said, "I raced with 145 cm poles. This year I used 160's until I broke one. Now I have 175's — it is a whole new concept." He points out that as you skate, the longer pole is in the snow for a longer time, resulting in more power. Some coaches use the formula of 2.3 times your height in inches to get the height of skating poles in centimeters. Borrow a pair of long poles and give them a try.

As racing equipment becomes more available, look for bargains in the stiff klister skis that, while not dubbed "skating skis," will serve you well for skating and better yet, allow a good wax pocket for diagonal stride. What better time to rely on a knowledgeable ski shop, one whose staff can steer you toward a multi-purpose equipment selection tailored to you.

SKATING AND RUNNING — PROBLEMS?

Skating on skis uses muscles in the thighs that you don't use in running; you direct pressure straight down the inside of the leg to the ski. After your first day of skating, you will feel it in the abductor muscles. You also may have sore arms and shoulders, especially if you skate with extra-long poles. You can do some specific training before the season to tone up your skating muscles. Serious racers practice skating on roller skis or training skates. Another system that some racers use is the slideboard — a system borrowed from speed skaters. Slideboards are simply a six to eight foot sheet of formica counter top (look in your discount lumber houses or talk to contractors who renovate kitchens) with padded sidewalls. Slide some wool socks over your shoes and you are in business. Push off with one leg, just like in skating, and slide to the opposite side of the board on your other foot. Some racers find that a spray can of furniture polish works better than talcum powder to keep the glide going. Some enterprising skaters note that nearly every home has a built-in slideboard, the bathtub. They put a little liquid soap in the bottom and glide back and forth on that. ("No ski poles in the tub," the sign says!)

It is easy to train for skating by modifying your running a bit. If you go out with poles to run hills in the fall, instead of charging straight up the hills, run diagonally back and forth across the slopes, bounding off the inner muscles. You can do the same with runs up stairs, running from side to side. "Take a few at a time," suggests ski instructor Jeanne Stopyro. "Make it more of a bounding type of motion."

Skating will pose a dilemma for some runners. Do we really want to develop muscles that might be antagonistic to running? The pelvic girdle muscles come into play as do the abductors. To some runners, the aerobic conditioning and change of pace will be worth the effort to skate, to others, the risk of "detraining" may make them stay with the diagonal stride, which is regarded as being more complementary to both running and biking.

Because skating is such a new technique among skiers, there has been little medical study done to establish whether any long term problems will develop. Among the Europeans, there have been reports of problems from skating. When Olympic Gold Medal winner Peter Angerer developed skating-related injuries at the start of the 1985 race season, sports writers in Germany described it as the "Curse of the Sittonen step." Several skiers on the Canadian Ski Team were bothered with compartment syndrome after the 1986 season.

Dr. Edward Hixson says that the reports are not in yet. "We don't have the answers yet. There are areas of potential problems which have been alluded to. There appear to be more problems with the arms with skating such as triceps tendinitis. There are, of course, the expected problems with chronic groin pulls, medial space knee pain as well as some medial foot difficulty."

For runners who want to take up skating, particularly those who want to do some racing, developing a few extra muscles in the legs and upper body won't be a worry. The twice a week runs will keep the running muscles tuned up and the gains in upper body strength may offset any "detraining" effects of skating. I like skating for aerobic training reasons. Without a lot of worry about snow temperatures and kick waxes or whether there are any tracks to ski in, I can be out the door on my glide-waxed skis in minutes. After a 45 minute workout of double-pole V-skate laps around a nearby field (snowmobile tracks work pretty well for skating), I come back dripping wet and tired, just as at the end of a hard five mile run. I've always had trouble getting that kind of quick workout from diagonal stride — that's why I skate.

Skating, once learned, is demanding, especially in the upper body, but it is a great way for a runner to get some speed on skis. It is a little like getting up on water skis for the first time — once you get the picture and the feeling locked in your mind, then it's just a matter of working at it and gaining experience. Talk to instructors and study the literature — skating is a rapidly evolving technique and there is no reason that runners can't learn the latest methods as soon as they are developed. And, as Swedish coach Kjell Kratz told a *CROSS COUNTRY SKIER* writer, "Once you learn to skate the right way and develop the proper rhythm, skating becomes the easiest, most natural motion. You feel like you can skate forever."

Some of the best skaters are the 15-year-olds who come into skiing with no hangups about technique. Runners are in a unique position because we also come to the sport with no preconceived notions as to what is right or wrong. We can learn these new techniques without having to "unlearn" anything. A ski coach told me, "If runners want to compete, they're going to want to skate. A person just starting out now is lucky, they are jumping into the sport when everybody else is in the same boat, learning to skate." Skating on skis is too much fun not to try.

Courtesy of Cross Country Canada

Young skiers find skating easy and fun.

6. Let's race

I had just shed my jacket and sweat-soaked polypropylene top when, with a swirl of snow and wind, my friend Bob crawled into the car. The windows steamed up as we both struggled into dry clothes, clothes that had been sitting in cold car for hours. As we munched on orange slices, drank from our water bottles, and waited for the car to warm up, he said, "You know, some folks would think that we're nuts. But this is great, isn't it?"

Most of the 300 skiers who, like us, had just completed the 15K cross country race on that cold, windy Saturday would have agreed. Some had driven five hours or more just to get to there. They, like us, had caught the fever of nordic racing.

Cross country ski racing is like running was a while back. Each season brings more events and more skiers giving local races a try. No longer for just a few devotees, nordic racing is gaining more attention and more participants. In fact, while road racing has leveled off and the number of runners in some races is dropping, nordic ski races, often called citizens' races or loppets, are growing in number. There is a place for everyone in most races. Hot skiers can whizz off at the front of the pack while their grandparents can take their time at the back. The mix of age and ability that makes so many local runs a family and social affair will likewise appeal to runners who decide to take up citizens' racing.

Whether you run a 10K race each weekend or just try a local "fun run" once a year, you can find a whole new competitive world in ski racing. You will find the same camaraderie and acceptance of newcomers that is prevalent in road racing. You also will find that there are new opportunities to win age group awards and to set new PRs.

TYPES OF RACES

There are two basic types of cross country races: the open race and the citizens's race. The open races are aimed at the competitive skier and may be strictly for one particular age group, say junior skiers. Racers are categorized by the U.S. Ski Association into four broad categories: Bill Koch Ski League (9-13), Juniors (13-19), Seniors (20-29), and Masters (30+). Open races will usually feature an interval start, where two skiers head out every 30 seconds. It is the way many of the Olympic and World Cup nordic races are held. Most of the racers at open races will be classified members although it is usually possible for other skiers to participate.

Be wary of open races — it is stiff competition and may not be suited for the novice racer. Don't be afraid to call the race organizer, explain your situation, and just ask if this is a race for you. If it looks like you'll be outclassed, try one of the citizens' races around where you will fit into the pack better. However, open races offer a great chance to watch good cross country skiers in action. It is fun to watch the ease with which they fly down the course and skate up the hills. It is a good chance for runners to find out exactly what techniques are being used by the top skiers. Find a

Courtesy of Douglas Reid

There's a place for everyone in citizens' racing.

race and watch it, you will be amazed.

Citizen ski racing is a lot like road racing was five years ago. Many of the races are low key, with inexperienced organizers, and nothing goes quite as planned. Some runners find skiers more abrasive, more testy when the gun goes off. The conflict between skaters and diagonal striders can also trigger boorish behavior. Yet, the spirit among most racers is just like you find at a local 10K on a Saturday morning. Many runners, once they get their skiing technique down, get hooked on citizens' racing. It's a great workout and lots of fun.

Finding ski races is not always easy. I've asked at good ski shops about upcoming races and got a blank look from the salesperson. You just don't find the sheaths of race applications around that you do for road racing — it is a much more closed operation, much more like bike racing in that respect. Even the ski magazines do not have race calendars. Check your ski shops, touring center, or local ski club.

In the U.S., a good source of information is the USSA. They put out a Nordic competitor's manual that lists every race in your section of the country. The price, for a beginner, is pretty steep ($35.00) but for that, you become a classified racer, get into some races at reduced fees, and get a subscription to a ski racing newsletter. I would borrow a manual from a racer the first year or so, then take the plunge and join up. In Canada, the provincial offices of Cross Country Canada (See Appendix) can steer you to both ski clubs as well as races in your area.

There are other ways to find out what's coming up for races. Ski club newsletters often list local races, some of the non-sanctioned events that are not on other schedules. Some clubs have race "hot lines" with recorded

Open races feature interval starts.

messages about upcoming events. One of the best ways to learn about future races is to ask other skiers after a race — you'll hear about some races you didn't know existed. For years, the ski race circuit was publicized by grapevine and it still pays to be tied into a network. Then when an event is changed to the following week due to lack of snow, you won't be driving hours to get to a non-existent race.

WHY DOES RACING COST SO MUCH?

It pays, literally, to find out where and when the races are. If you are interested in entering an open race, you usually will have to pre-register because there is a cutoff date several days before the race. (The entries are seeded for the interval start so there is no day-of-race registration.) Many mass start citizens' races allow you to sign up on race day, but like in road racing, there is often a pretty stiff penalty. Unlike road racing, early registration is a gamble, especially if the season is marginal due to snow conditions. If you pay early, a January thaw may wipe out the race and along with it, your entry fee. But, if you wait, you pay more. This becomes even more critical in major marathon ski races, where the fees often double or triple as race day nears.

If you have complained about the escalating entry fees in road running, you will be shocked by the prices in many ski races. Race entry fees in skiing are high and you don't get much for your money, just a good race. No T-shirts, biking caps, or sweatbands — the types of gee-gaws that runners expect for a $10-15 fee. The larger races hand out pins or medals, but the entry fees are higher, starting in the $25 (or more) range and climbing to twice that for later entries.

Trail grooming is an expensive part of race course preparation.

Putting ski races on is costly business: there is a little more to it than getting the sheriff to block off a few roads. Ski touring centers don't foot the bill for many races because they can make more money, in a short season, doing other things. Therefore, most citizens' races fall upon the ski clubs — which have very limited resources to start with. A mid-West U.S. club newsletter explained the costs of their race like this: "Many skiers ask about the actual cost of the cross country ski race. The following is a list of most of the ... expenses: $1 head tax per skier (up to $200) to the USSA, $100 to the U.S. Forest Service for a race permit, $200-500 for portable toilets, $300 postage, $500 paper and printing, $400-$500 for medals, $150 for plaques, $300-$500 for racing bibs, $150 for refreshments, $100 for office expenses, $100 for rental of timers, $1000 for miscellaneous expenses such as signs, flags, banners, insurance, bus rental, gasoline, heaters, first aid kits, badges, ski stickers, and $1000 for bulldozing and grooming/track-setting equipment."

BEFORE THE RACE

Ski races, whether a local winter carnival race or big name event, have the same atmosphere that 10k road races do. Get to a race in plenty of time — you not only have to get yourself ready but you need to get your equipment ready to go. Local race groups are often neophytes, and registration may be painfully slow. The hubbub is compounded by racers try to wax, change into clothing, and stay warm before the race.

If you've ever been amazed by some of the pre-race nervous energy that comes out in road races — the exotic stretches, the yoga stances, the high-stepping sprints of the elite runners, you'll love to people-watch at citizens' races. Skiers race in everything from plaid hunting coats (with the license pinned on the back) to slick form-fitting racing suits that would have been banned in Boston not many years ago. You'll see old wooden touring skis to the latest high-tech results of the ski labs. But don't be fooled by appearances, some of the "traditionalists" who shun the glitzy equipment are very good skiers — I know, I've been passed by a few in the last kilometers of a race.

Most ski races will have a warming area where you can do some last minute waxing. Here's where you will hear some of the same hype and white lies you hear at road races — people discussing their training programs, which if you listen, sound like pre-Olympic routines. "Yeah, I put in an easy week: an easy 30K Sunday, some hill work, and a race Wednesday night." Watch out for those who say, "I'm really not in shape yet, I'm going to use this as a training run." Sports psyching takes many forms.

When you are new to the citizens' racing scene, the waxing routines are interesting to watch. In one corner, a skier is wrestling with a tube of blue klister while nearby, a front-runner sets up a portable waxing bench, opens a box holding an array of wax which looks like an organic chemistry lab. I'm always reminded of the weekend bass fisherman and his four-tray tackle box with 25 pounds of lures. He probably really only uses a couple of favorites. The same holds true for many skiers — if they skate, they use only a few types of glide wax; the rest of the paraphernalia is a security blanket. If you look at their waxes, several will be nearly gone while most others are untouched. Watch good skiers wax their skis, you can learn a lot from them.

The attitudes of cross country skiers toward newcomers is great. I have

Courtesy of Tug Hill Tourathon, Inc.

Citizens' races have many older skiers.

never felt like I was invading a clique. People seem glad to share information about waxing, trouble spots on the course — it is a very supportive atmosphere, and a good reason to arrive early. Ask around to see if there are any top racers at your race, chances are you won't know them by sight. Elite racers are much more accessible than elite runners, mainly because the sport is that much smaller, and skiers mingle without being paid to do it.

It is often hard to figure out what to wear out on the course — it is easy to wear too much. You will be surprised at how warm you get once you get moving and how much fluid you lose. Take your lead from other racers. You can race with a light fanny pack and carry a light shell or extra hat in it — you will never notice the extra weight.

You will not see much stretching before the race. Warm up and stretch as you would for a road race. Go for a short run in your cross country boots, then warm up a little on skis to check the conditions. Stay warm just before the race by jogging in place. Race organizers never seem to have enough water available at the start of a race. Bring your own just to be sure and drink several glasses, up to 32 ounces, in the hour before the race. Just as in road racing, you will have to balance your intake versus outgo by judicious timing of visits to the latrines. (It is a slower process with several layers and zippers to contend with.)

THE START

If you like friendly chaos, you'll love mass starts at citizens' races. Until you have raced a while, it will be a little hard to seed yourself, not knowing how fast you'll ski. Don't make the mistake of starting too far back because you will expend too much energy trying to pass slower racers. Look for people who look like they are about the same caliber. For me, that turns out to be behind those in color-coordinated outfits who look like they are out for blood but ahead of those who are having trouble standing up in the start area. Get in place early and sort of spread out a bit, sticking your poles in on each side, staking out a claim.

Just like in a road race, too many people line up too far in front and nearly get trampled in the first rush. Take it easy, keep your balance, remember that there's a lot of race ahead, and the race will soon settle down as skiers find their own pace and niche.

If you skate, and believe me, you will after your first few races, be ready to double pole the first kilometer. Many races, trying to avoid interference problems, ban skating in the first K. If you only have glide wax on, you will have to double pole. Use short power strokes and skate as soon as you can.

If you are kick waxing (Chapter 10), you will know by the first mile if your wax is right for the snow conditions. When checking wax beforehand, remember that the tracks will become even more packed and glazed by the skiers ahead of you. Because of this, you'll tend to slip more than you want, especially later in the race as the wax wears off.

SKIING THE RACE

Racing protocol calls for passing on the left if there are two tracks and stepping aside, if there is only one. There is a lot of passing, especially during the first 5K of shorter races. Some skiers are better climbers than others, some better on the flats, people ski in spurts and then slow down — it is much more noticeable than in running. Most people passing are polite, saying or yelling "track" or "on the left" to let you know that they want to pass.

Generally, unless you are skating, you should ski in the right lane if it is not too rutted, especially if skiers are coming up behind you. Take your time changing tracks, the guy or gal coming up can wait. This is no time to fall.

Watch out for the first downhill, that is where the pileups start. One of the race courses that I ski quite frequently has a tough downhill at about the 5K mark. In the middle of the pack, the race grinds to a halt at this point as skiers line up and wait their turn to "run the gauntlet." It is quite a sight the first time — skiers howl as they rip down the hill and then take a spill at the bottom, people fall right in front of you as you madly maneuver to miss them, others, probably the runners, say, "Forget this," and take off their skis and jog down the hill. Others sit on their ski tails and slide down. If you are a novice skier, you'll probably encounter a few situations like this. Don't worry, make up the lost time on the flats.

Going downhill, try to maintain a safe distance behind the person in front, and hope that everyone stays upright. After you get to the bottom, keep moving — that is where it is easy to get plowed into by someone from behind and get knocked down, after you have made it down safely. When you fall, get your skis and poles out of the track. Roll over to the side and wait for a good opening before starting out again.

It is easy to get going too fast and lose control. It takes practice and leg muscles to hold a good snowplow on a steep downhill. You can feel it in the quads as you press to keep the edges dug in. If you are in double tracks, use one ski to snowplow to maintain control Many skiers tire, relax the wedge, and start moving down the hill too fast. Be ready for icy, semi-bare hills to snowplow on — don't forget, many racers ahead of you have already dug in and scraped snow away. Before long, you'll welcome downhills as a breather.

Uphills, especially those early in the race, are also potential bottlenecks. The leaders glide right up the hills but further back, the pace slows. It actually can be a chance to catch your breath and relax, even though you are climbing. The slow herringbone ascents are a good place to use your running strength. What you may lack in technique you may make up in conditioning.

Problems on uphills are often caused by the people ahead. Just as you shift from diagonal to a herringbone, you have to stop when folks up ahead run out of gas. Keep at it, keep your weight forward and your poles in action, and as you crest the hill, just as you try to do in running, pass the skiers who are exhausted by the climb.

Hills can be bottlenecks during the race.

If you are on a looped course and have fast skiers in the race, you may get lapped. Al Merrill, former Olympic coach and international racing expert says, "Skating presents real interference problems. You can't believe how fast the elite skiers go — it's tough to get out of their way. Say you're doing the herringbone on a hill — it is difficult to move in time."

As the race goes on, you can expect to have the tracks pretty well chewed up by the racers ahead, especially where the course is narrow. Most races have skating on the left and diagonal stride on the right. Skaters try to stay out of the tracks, unless they are marathon skating, yet you will have to contend with a chewed-up course for some of the way. (All the more reason to take up skating.)

Ski racing is a great place to work on technique, trying to be as efficient as possible. Watch others who are good and imitate them. Relax, don't grip your poles tightly, and work on the diagonal stride. I shake my hands every so often, just as I do on the roads, to sort of loosen my arms and hands. Use your aerobic conditioning on the flats and the slight inclines where you'll be most efficient at first as a runner/skier.

Drink water in the race whenever you can. Many shorter races don't have water stops but if they do, take fluids. Expect to receive lukewarm water or sweet GatorAid or KoolAid. Even though it is cold, you need the fluids. Studies have shown that elite skiers lose 3.4 pounds of water in a 20K race. In marathons, you can lose up to 13 pounds of water. Just as in road racing, you have to replace that water before you get thirsty. Pass up the sweet sticky liquids that race organizers love unless you are sure that your stomach can handle it — drink water if it is available. It is more readily absorbed by your system.

As the race progresses, you may feel a bit unsteady. The simplest downhill can present problems late in the race. Concentrate on technique and try to ski smoothly. As you approach the finish, avoid last minute sprints — this is no time to fall. You have tired legs — stay as efficient as possible and finish smoothly, noting your time.

After the race, get some fluids and food and climb into something warm and dry (before too many races, you will learn new techniques for getting dressed and undressed in your car), and go out and swap stories with the other finishers. This is a good time to check on upcoming races and talk with skiers about other courses and other races. Some stretches should be part of your post-race routine. Take a moment to jot down not only your time and any splits that you can remember, but anything unique about the race that will help you ski even a better race next year. Because you will be back.

7. Let's tour

Long before cross country ski centers began to dot the countryside, skiers were enjoying the specialness of ski touring. This "do-it-yourself" aspect of cross country skiing is what draws thousands of people to the sport each year. It is a chance to shed some of the trappings of a regimented lifestyle and enjoy the winter outdoors — and get some exercise in the bargain.

Some runners will want to compete on skis, but others are looking for a break from the road racing scene. Ski touring provides "participation" in place of "competition." Whether it is an outing on the local golf course, a few loops around the local touring center, or a backwoods day hike, ski touring provides a leisurely workout for the runner. It can be like heading out for an easy Saturday morning run with friends, leaving the watch at home, just running easily. Ski touring provides the chance to enjoy the company of family and friends and the special world of winter. The stillness of a winter morning — trees creaking in the sharp air — the pleasure of watching your ski tips plow through fresh powder snow, showering snow crystals in the sunlight — the pleasures of stopping on the trail for lunch — are some of the reasons that touring is so popular.

There are many cross country skiers who could care less about offset

V-skating, Boron racing poles, Lycra one-piece suits, or groomed trails and set tracks. That's not cross country skiing to them. Some are converts from the alpine skiing scene — escapees from the costs, the ski lift lines, and the "glitz" of downhill skiing. Ski touring has none of the trappings of trendiness — it is a chance to wear old clothes, go out when you want to, and for as long as you want.

Runners have a chance to sample all sides of cross country skiing. With the aerobic base that they bring to the sport, they can, as was noted in the last chapter, jump into low-key citizens' races or loppets and enjoy the chance to compete in a new sport. On the other hand, with the same set of skis, boots, and poles, they can "do their own thing" and never get near other skiers or organized events. It is this flexibility that makes cross country skiing such a popular sport. You can go out and ski tour all day and there is no entry fee. It is one of the best aerobic bargains around.

WHERE TO GO

Ski touring usually involves skiing at a leisurely pace — it is more like walking or hiking than running. Carrying a small pack with a lunch and drinks, you can tour for hours at a time and feel pleasantly tired at the end of the day. When learning to ski, it is easier to tour at facilities that have groomed trails and set tracks. Many of these sites not only have extensive networks of trails, they also grade the trails according to difficulty. This way, a novice can concentrate on technique and enjoy the outing — there's no need to be concerned about getting lost or about how tough the trail is up ahead. Even so, most ski tourers would rather shun the tracks and the other skiers. They want to get away from the warming huts and the

Ski touring allows you to enjoy family and friends and the special world of winter.

groomed trails and strike out on an adventure. It might be an outing with friends, skiing down an old logging road for a hot dog cookout, or even a week-long expedition with full camping gear. For most runners, ski tours will be day trips — a "let's pack up and tour for a while" type of outing. You can do that nearly anywhere there's snow.

Short local ski tours — the trip to the county or provincial park, the school grounds, or the golf course — are good chances to get experience for longer outings. You can learn what to take, how fast to ski to fit the pace to the group, and whether you want to tackle more ambitious outings. The next step may be to try a tour on some rural farmland or woodlots, perhaps using existing snowmobile trails. Don't assume that open land is "free" for skiing, even if it's not posted. Take the time to ask permission. There's nothing more maddening to a farmer, who may have just received a whopping property tax bill in the January mail, to have a carload of skiers pile out and troop out across the pasture without asking. It is just common courtesy; most landowners don't mind having skiers using their land.

WHAT TO WEAR

Ski touring is like touring on a bike — it is not a mad dash from point to point — rather, it is a chance to observe, to appreciate the winter scenery around us. The pace is steady enough to keep warm but not fast enough to break into a heavy sweat. Because of the pace, you need a little more clothing than you might for a concentrated ski workout.

As in any skiing, dress in layers, all of them light. Most ski tourers think in terms of three layers. First comes a layer of long underwear of one of the new materials such as Polypropelene, Capeline, or TRP. (You want something to wick any perspiration away from the body.) Next, an insulating layer is worn, especially on the upper body. This might be a light wool sweater or a turtleneck made from a new material such as Polarfleece. You'll find that your legs will usually stay warm without an insulating layer. The outer layer is the wind-proofing, weather-repellent layer. Here is where a winter running suit is perfect. Some skiers will wear jeans as a layer — most shy away from them because of the possibilities of chafing, especially when the denim gets wet.

Most beginners dress too warmly, get sweaty during the first climb, and then get chilled. It takes experience to find out what works for you; it is an individual matter. Ski tour on the cool side, keeping an extra shell stuffed in a fanny pack in case the weather changes. Add a hat and mittens (which are warmer than gloves), and you are ready to roll. If there is a lot of snow, gaiters are helpful to keep the snow out of your boots. Protect your eyes from the sun with sunglasses, and use skin cream and chapstick.

WHAT TO BRING

If you are out for a backyard tour in the local park, there is little else you need. If you wax, throw a couple of tins of grip wax into your pocket and bring a scraper. Orange slices in a zip bag are easy to stow, and if there's clean snow, they taste great dipped in snow. Apples slices also are easy snacks to bring.

For longer tours, you need to be better prepared, not only so that you can enjoy a lunch on the trail, but so that you can deal with any unexpected problems. A fanny pack or small backpack is often used to carry food and clothing. Here are some of the things that you should consider having along

on any trip outside the local park or touring center:
   An extra pair of white wool socks
   A garbage bag (for emergency windbreaking)
   An extra ski tip (lug one and you'll probably never need it)
   A small first aid kit
   Swiss Army knife
   A couple of screws for bindings
   Compass and map
   Candle, waterproof matches
   A whistle
   Extra clothing
   Trail snacks (raisins, oranges, apples, cheese & crackers)
   Water bottle
Looking at the list, it looks as if we are going to trek across wilderness areas and need all our Boy Scout or Girl Scout survival skills to do it. Actually, ski touring is pretty tame, yet, anyone can get a little turned around. Likewise, any runner who has been caught out on a long run by a sudden storm knows how easy is is to get tricked by a weather change on the ski trail. That 40 degree sunny day can go to a wind chill of minus 40 when a cold front passes. It never hurts to play it safe, to be prepared. Put the gear into a little sack, stash it in your fanny pack when you're ready to go, and you'll probably never need it.

   Tour with others, don't get off on your own. Usually, three skiers are considered a minimum — then if someone gets hurt, one can stay and one can ski out for help. Before you start out, let someone know where you are going and how long you will be gone.

DAY TRIPS

While one of the attractions of ski touring is its free-form nature, there are some things to keep in mind when you're going out all day. We already covered the items to go in the pack, now let's review some other basics.

Planning — It is a good idea to check the route over beforehand with a topographical map, especially if you don't have someone along who knows the area. If you are not too sharp on reading contour lines, this pre-ski study gives you a chance to learn or dust off map reading skills. You can spot potential trouble areas — marshy spots that might not be frozen over, steep hills, or streams and rivers that might need to be crossed. If you are just going out to a neighbor's woodlot, you obviously can do without a map. However, if you are planning to ski in unfamiliar territory, the small investment in a map is worth it.

Out and back trips are the most common. If there is new snow, you get to take advantage of the tracks you made on the way in. Loops let you explore new terrain all the way. One way trips require logistic planning — someone needs to leave a car at both ends of the tour.

For many runners, ski touring planning will consist of, "It's a great day, let's load up the skis and go." With a few provisions, you are off on an outing. The spontaneity of touring is one of its charms. It can be spoiled by too much planning.

Hitting the Trail — Pick a safe place to park the car. If you are parking at a trailhead, leave the vehicle so that the snowplows don't bury it. Don't block farm roads or woods roads — remember, loggers and farmers work on weekends. Aim the car out of the wind so that you don't return to an engine compartment filled with snow. Check that the headlights are off.

Whether racing or touring, bridge crossings can be challenging.

How about spare keys? A set should be left attached to the bumper in a magnetic case.

It is a good idea to leave food and drinks in the car. Water in a plastic water bottle won't freeze unless you are skiing in arctic conditions. High energy food like brownies and cookies are great to come back to. You will have earned a decadent snack.

Setting the Pace — This is not interval training. Don't be an obnoxious runner with too much energy. Most likely there's a mixed bag of athletic ability and conditioning along — set the pace to keep everyone together. Don't try to use a ski tour in place of a running workout — you'll just be frustrated and also end up with some unhappy skiing companions. Get your kinks out ahead of time with a quick morning run or else just use the tour day as a rest day. (You won't gain 20 pounds and suffer any detraining effect; in fact it'll probably be good for you.)

Touring can give you a pleasantly tired feeling at the end of the day, but you probably won't be getting your heart rate up into the aerobic zone. You can squeeze in a little extra work anyway — carry the heaviest pack, offer to break the trail, ski up ahead to check out spots for lunch. If you are leading, be sensitive to the others by making sure that no one is over-taxed and too proud to say "slow down for a minute." Take some breaks for snacks or to admire a view; this is an outing, not a forced march.

Along the Trail — Some of the most interesting parts of tours are the crossings, the streams, the fences, and the roads that must be crossed. If you are traversing a wet area, be alert for icing on your skis. Slide the skis forcefully along, trying not to lift them, wiping them clean on the drier snow after the crossing. Even so, you might check the bottoms. In half a minute you can scrape any ice or mud off and save lots of energy.

Bridges provide interesting challenges for ski tourers. Many are planked bridges with slats and gaps which are notorious for catching ski poles or skis. If the bridge looks too challenging, take your skis off and walk. The same goes for fences. Barbed wire and P-Tex bases seem to have an attraction. If you have to cross fences, it may pay to take off your skis, even if you sink into the snow. Be careful because wood and barbed wire are brittle in the cold. Don't inadvertently snap a strand by standing on it.

Lunch on the Trail — Eating can be an ongoing activity while skiing — some raisins to nibble, some orange slices, even cookies — all make the kilometers more enjoyable. It's a side of skiing that runners aren't used to, but it's an easy habit to pick up. You're earning those calories.

Meals on a tour can be anything from the backpackers GORP (good old raisins and peanuts) to a full-blown meat and potatoes stew. Most skiers, unless on a long tour with backpack gear, opt for snacks and drinks. Sandwiches and a thermos of hot chocolate often fit the bill.

What about open fire cookouts? Picture a group of toasty-warm skiers, grouped around a campfire, warm food in their stomachs, smiles for one another. Right out of a Miller beer commercial, right? Now picture a smoldering collection of wet sticks, four raw hot dogs struggling to decide whether to freeze or thaw in the smoke, and several "getting colder, every minute" skiers wondering why they ever bothered to stop to eat, and you've got another side of lunch on the trail. By all means, if you are experienced in the woods, find a sheltered spot, clear the snow away, and construct a fire to cook on. If you're going to give it a try, carry some tinder from home, some paper and dry kindling. Use the wood already down and dead and

Lunch on the trail can be fun.

keep the fire reasonable in size. Clean up the area before you go and double check that the fire is out.

If you are serious about cookouts, a small propane stove used in hiking may be the best bet. It can heat liquids fast and is light and reliable. It gets the job done without all the smoke and sarcasm.

Drink plenty of liquids while touring. Even though you are not perspiring heavily, you still need replacement fluids. You are also losing water through respiration. Remember that last run in really cold conditions, how your face mask or hat was covered with ice? It's all from water lost from breathing. Dehydration comes easily when skiing — and the loss of water can make you more susceptible to frostbite. Hydrate before the tour and drink often — water bottles are a good addition to a fanny pack.

Some skiers will carry wineskins on a tour. Be cautious, it's a little like carrying wine in your bike bottles — it sure doesn't help the balance. Just as important, alcohol is a depressant and can be dangerous in cold conditions. It dilates the blood vessels which lets the skin lose heat faster, leading to potential frostbite problems.

A Safe Return — Days are short in December and January and it pays to head back out in plenty of time to clear the trails by dark. The trip will probably be slower on the way back out due to tired legs and arms. The tour should end with a feeling of, "I could have skied another hour."

HANDLING TROUBLE

While we don't have to deal with nasty dogs, pickup trucks, or heat exhaustion while cross country skiing, we do face some of the same problems that we encounter while running.

Getting Lost — Ever been lost while running in a strange city, in subdivisions where every street and house look alike? Or gotten into sections of town where you are probably not welcome? Generally, while you can get disoriented while running in new territory, it is just a matter of asking directions from a passerby. Not so in the woods.

If you tour in rural country or wilderness areas, you should have someone along that knows how to use a map and compass, and you'd better have the map and compass with you. There is little chance of getting lost on many tours — you can just follow your ski tracks back out. But, tracks can be obliterated by new snow, snow machines, or other skiers, and believe me, you can find your tracks and still be so turned around that you can not tell which way is out.

Winter survival is covered in many of the skiing and mountaineering books on the market but there are some basics that runners should know — the four C's — Climb, Confess, Conserve, Communicate.

Climb — If the weather is clear and you have the time and energy, climb a hill and look around. Compare what you see with your map. Look for prominent landmarks — rivers, villages, antennas. Don't head out until you are sure of the direction.

Confess — admit that you are lost, call it "turned around" if you like. Say it out loud, to yourself, to your group. Then deal with the problem.

Conserve — Save your energy until you have a plan worked out — don't burn calories by getting panicked. If darkness is near, consider spending the night and start gathering some materials for a shelter. (Unless you are experienced, forget about digging a snow cave — they take good snow conditions and are difficult to construct unless you've done it a few times.) Button up your clothing to retain body heat and restrict your movements. Check around for a sheltered spot — an old log with some space under it, a rock outcropping, a cave. Get out of the wind any way you can. If there is no natural shelter to improve, dig a snow trench with your ski tips. You and your friends, with skis, poles, and boughs to cover the shelter and evergreen boughs for ground cover, can huddle together out of the elements, tell funny running stories ("There I was with a Doberman hanging off my shorts and the owner yelling, 'Don't worry, he won't bite!' ") and wait for daylight.

Communicate — That whistle in your pack can be heard for a good distance. Don't be shy about yelling. Don't spend a lot of energy tromping out snow signals or preparing massive bonfires; that's ok in the movies but takes too much energy. Folks will most likely be looking for you on snowmobiles and skis — with airplanes later on.

Whether you stay put or travel when lost depends a lot on your situation and your expertise. If you've let people know where you were going, someone will be looking for you soon.

FROSTBITE AND HYPOTHERMIA

Runners who hit the roads in winter probably have dealt with frostbite or the early stages of it. When your fingers get numb and jaundiced-looking and sting when warmed up, that's incipient frostbite. Frostbite is usually caused by wind chill. It is even easier to suffer frostbite while skiing, even if the wind isn't blowing, due to the speed involved, especially on the downhills. There are times when you can just feel the wind cut through your clothing. That's when I stuff some plastic or newspaper down into my crotch and try to be alert to the potential of frostbite.

Protect exposed skin with creams or a face mask and wear a hat which covers the ears. Heat loss from exposed skin can happen fast, especially when you are skiing downhill. Warm the extremities before they get too cold. Sometimes, you'll find that the hands get cold before getting too far on a tour, before you get the body really warmed up. If you can get you hands warm by putting them in your armpits (That'll get your attention!), you can often ski the rest of the day without problems.

Frostbite does not hurt at first. The early warning signs of frostbite, aside from a numb tingly feeling, is a whitish look on the frost-bitten area. Have others skiers check for you. Warm up any frostbitten areas — put an ungloved hand over white skin for minor frostbite. You will be ok if the color returns but keep checking it. Deep frostbite requires medical attention — don't try to thaw it out, get the skier to immediate medical attention.

Hypothermia is something that most tour skiers will never encounter or even think about — yet is is worth knowing about because it is so dangerous. It is basically freezing to death — lowering the temperature of the body's core.

It doesn't take sub-freezing temperatures to suffer from hypothermia. Ever finished a marathon on a cool day and gotten chilled before you got into dry clothes? That shivering, "looking like a ghost" feeling that comes from being exhausted and chilled is the onset of hypothermia. It is why "space blankets" are handed out after the major marathons.

Hypothermia is insidious, it can sneak up on you. Watch for signs of uncontrolled shivering, loss of coordination, or sluggishness among skiers on a tour. If someone has the symptoms, get them warmed up, get their body

Spring is the favorite time to tour for many skiers.

temperature up, and feed them warm food and liquids. Use extra layers of clothing and if there's a sleeping bag around, wrap up the person and have one of the group get in as well. Body to body heat has saved many a hypothermia patient.

Snacking along the way, keeping warm and dry, and skiing within your ability — that's how to prevent hypothermia.

TOURING = FUN

After describing how much freedom and fun comes from touring, and how thousands of skiers around the world enjoy getting out on ski tours, we then bring up all the potential problems — getting lost, frostbite, hypothermia — it's enough to keep one back at the warming hut by the fire. Let me reassure you, touring is one of the safest outdoor activities there is. For runners, there are no vehicles to dodge, no overuse injuries to nag, no high heart rates to tax the system.

A veteran ski tourer put it like this, "I am 67 years old and have enjoyed cross country skiing since before it became a popular sport here in Minnesota. I was out there in my beautiful world, mostly by myself, making my own trails, stopping to enjoy the snowy scenes, taking photos or bird watching with the binoculars I always had with me. A snack in my backpack extended my stay in places where I wished I could remain forever...."

The camaraderie of friends, the chance to get out with the family for the day, the warm, tired feeling at the end of the tour as you share stories over stew or spaghetti — these are the "perks" of ski touring.

8. Masters racing

We were standing next to a couple of teenage runners at an informal awards ceremony after a local 10K in Vermont. As age group awards were being handed out, the race director noted the finishing place and time. The young man beside me leaned to his partner and said, "Boy, these old guys are pretty fast."

The fast and not-so-fast men and women of masters age comprise one of the strongest movements in road running. Runners like Barry Brown, Antonio Villanueva, and Priscilla Welch are right up there with the front runners. Competition is fierce in most of the 40 and over age groups, and each year, a new crop of good runners graduates to masters racing. So it also is with cross country skiing.

In the 1986 Lake Placid Loppett 50 kilometer race, the top six skiers out of the field of 200 were masters skiers, men in their thirties and forties. In the women's field, second place went to a 45-49 age group skier. Just as in road racing, masters ski racing is coming into its own. Younger master skiers are winning races while others in their fifties and sixties finish high in the pack. Sometimes they win. The Inland Empire Ski Club newsletter described a 30K race like this: "One of those Norwegians with an older face on a young body, Einer Svenson, 59 years young, came out from Seattle and smoked everyone. His time was eight minutes ahead of anyone else." The writer, tongue in cheek, echoed many skiers when she continued, "... I can't wait to get older so I can ski like that."

Masters racing kindles a competitive spark in many masters skiers. Dr. John Bland put it like this, "I am in my 68th year and the best is yet to come." Bland recovered from a heart attack nine years before and goes on to report that he now plays basketball, football, "in fact any sport, all playfully except running and cross country skiing — when I get a bib on, I seem to grow fangs!"

This competitive enthusiasm has made masters skiing the fastest growing segment of the cross country scene. Masters racing starts at age thirty in skiing, which is a surprise to many runners who are accustomed to competing against the over-forty group. Many of the top skiers in the lower age range compete in open meets against high school and college-aged skiers and also clean up in masters competition. Age classes are set in 5-year increments by the USSA. Masters races have nine age groups: 30-34, 35-39, 40-44, 45-49, 50-54, 55-59, 60-64, 65-69, and 70 & up. The older age groups were added in 1984 because, as USSA's Lee Todd put it, "We've got people moving into their 70s, and they didn't want to be competing against one of those 60-year-old 'kids.' " As in running, the smaller ski races tend to have 10-year age groups while the larger go with 5 year increments.

Most citizens' races have a good sprinkling of older skiers, more so than in running. The level of competition is much like running — if you have several runners in your age group that consistently beat you, fear not, you will probably have a like number of skiers ready and waiting to trounce

you. But there is a wide range of ability. At one end of the spectrum, there are former national ski team members who haven't lost much in conditioning or technique, high school and college coaches who train and ski with their athletes, and Scandinavians who grew up on skis.

In the middle of the pack, the majority of masters skiers are less accomplished but sometimes just as competitive. There are some spirited age group battles as skiers, many of whom have dueled each other for years, go at it once again. Others race because they like the chance to compete against themselves, to set PRs, in some cases, just to finish. In big races like the Great American Ski Chase series, these masters men and women, 30 to 50 in age, make up the biggest number of participants. Masters runners who take up skiing will, if they chose to race, find that they are jumping into an active stream of energetic folks. Runners who learn to skate and develop good technique will find that they can do well in masters competition.

Who makes up the back of the pack in ski races? Folks who like to ski tour and enter a few races a year, skiers who are new to the sport, or not in great condition, or both. There's room at citizens' races for all masters skiers — it is as open as most local road races.

Open races, while sometimes set up with masters age groups as well, often have a race for juniors and a race for seniors. There may be a couple of masters classes tagged on such as 30-45, and over 45. If you are over 40 and like me, not too keen about racing against hot 30-year-olds and ski coaches, you may find yourself a little out-classed. It is sometimes better to go and watch or help out — I like to stand by a coach and listen up. You can pick up a lot of pointers, especially on skating, just by watching.

Aside from open races and citizens' races, there are also a growing number of races either aimed right at masters, or which include masters competition as a major part of the race.

MASTERS RACE SERIES

Since the late 1970s, masters ski racing has blossomed in the United States through the formation of the Great American Ski Chase, whose races have masters age group awards, and in Canada through the establishment of the Canadian Masters Association. Masters racing has flourished in both countries through the establishment of several regional race series. These masters series are not always special races just for masters, they are often citizens' races with masters scoring — sort of a race within a race. Here are some of the major North American series for masters.

The Zak Cup is a series of masters races sponsored by the Eastern Division of USSA. First known as the Eastern Veterans' Cup, it was named for the late Dr. Vlastimil Zak, who epitomized the spirit and camaraderie of masters racing. The Zak series had over a dozen races during its first years, but now has settled in at four races, at distances from 10k to 50K. The races are held in New Hampshire, Vermont, Maine, and New York, and awards are given to men and women winners in each 10 year age group. Skiers have to ski three of the four events to qualify and points are awarded according to the World Cup point system for the first fifteen in each age group. Age group leaders are named to the Eastern Masters Cross Country Team.

Also in the eastern U.S., the New York State Ski Racing Association conducts an extensive state-wide series of Empire State Games masters races that culminate in a 25K championship race in Lake Placid in March. Skiers are scored by age group for any three masters series races and then the

Stand by a coach and listen — you're bound to pick up some tips.

championship race results, weighted twice as heavily, are added. This race series is gaining rapidly in popularity.

In Massachusetts, masters championship races, open to state residents, are held at the Bay State Games. Masters races are held at the 15K and 20K distances.

The Laurel Highlands Ski Touring Association, a volunteer organization serving skiers in Pennsylvania, Maryland, and West Virginia, organizes the Allegheny Mountain Race Series which consists of a dozen races, ranging from 8K to 15K. While not strictly a masters series, the races have an age group for masters who are 40 years and older. Age group scoring is done using a points system (26 for first, 22 for 2nd, down to 1 for twentieth), and the best six races are counted for each racer.

The Central Division of the United States Ski Association sponsors a master race series in the upper mid-West (Michigan, Minnesota, Wisconsin). Skiers must compete in a least 2 of the qualifying races as well as the Central Masters Championship race. The top ranked skiers in each age group are named to the Central Masters Team.

A new entrant in USSA masters series racing is the Rocky Mountain Masters Series which is held at different sites in Colorado.

U.S. National Masters Championships are held each year. Events are 30/20K, 15/10K, and 3 X 10/5 relays (Women ski the shorter distances). An honorary U.S. masters ski team is chosen from those who compete in the two individual events. Usually the series is held near and just before a major 50K race which serves as an added attraction.

The Canadian Masters Cross-country Association likewise conducts regional masters competitions and a Canadian National Championship.

Master series races are growing in number as more masters athletes from other sports take up cross country skiing and as more former open skiers decide that they would like something a little less demanding and competitive. There is a wide range of abilities and experience and in most races, the only qualifications are to be age 30 or more and to pay the entry fee.

WORLD MASTERS

Up until recently, there were few places where masters skiers, unless you were really in shape and competitive and wanted to enter some of the open meets (and race against folks young enough to be your son or daughter), could compete. Much of the drive for masters racing at the international level began in Canada after an inaugural race in 1980. Bill Gairdner, a former Olympic decathlon athlete turned skier, put together a Canadian masters organization. Rejecting the term "veteran" as demeaning, Gairdner found strong support for a masters group. "...we decided that sport retains its highest meaning throughout the entire span of one's life," he explains, "and that even though aging is universal, the striving for excellence is ageless, and deserves respect regardless of one's physical age. In other words, a champion at any age is still a champion."

In the U.S., a sister group was set up by another energetic masters skier, Tom Duffy. Both organizations have flourished and now have over 500 members each. (It is a bargain at $12.00 — $10 in Canada.)

Duffy says that U.S. members range from college professors to woodcarvers and come from all over the United States as well as England and Australia. He feels that the biggest reason to have the World Masters organization "is the opportunity for masters skiers to meet and compete

World Masters Championships bring out keen competition in every age group.

against each other annually, and to try to achieve each of our personal goals, whether it is to win our age division, or to finish the race in what each feels is our personal best time."

World Masters Cross-Country Ski Championships are now held each year and rotate annually between North America, Scandinavia, and Europe. Races are held at 10/15K, 20/30K, 30/50K distances as well as a relay race. When the series is held in North America, the races also serve as the USA-Canada Cup Challenge Series, a competition between U.S. and Canadian masters.

It is exciting, and humbling, for most North American masters skiers to race against their peers from across the world. The level of competition is keen but yet, any masters skier can enter a World Masters meet. Talent ranges from ex-Olympians to "to finish is to win" skiers. Many Canadian and U.S. masters skiers who competed in the 1986 races at Lake Placid's Mt. Van Hovenburg were pushed to new PRs.

The World Masters schedule is:

1987 — Kuusamo, Finland	1990 — Ostersund, Sweden
1988 — Seefeld, Austria	1991 — Toblack, Italy
1989 — Canada	

Masters racing, whether at the local level or the World Masters level, is coming into its own. It represents a great opportunity for runners to compete against skiers in their own age group. Just as importantly, it gives one a chance to rub elbows with an interesting group of runners, bikers, walkers, canoeists, kayakers, and triathletes who use skiing as a second sport. But watch out, you'll also meet grandfathers and grandmothers who, as Dr. Bland says, "grow fangs when they put racing bibs on."

9. Ski 31 miles?

The alarm rings at 3:00 AM. You pile into the car and are on the road by 3:30, facing a five hour drive, to be there by a 9:00 AM start, ready to ski 50K. Who else but runners do such nutty things? Why skiers, of course. (And bikers, canoeists, and triathletes, to name a few.)

Marathon skiing has all the trappings of marathon running — the logistics of getting to the race, long lines at check-in, a crowded mass start, and the camaraderie among competitors. Ski marathons range from international happenings with thousands of competitors to local loppets with attendance in the hundreds. Lengths are not standard although most are generally 50 or 55 kilometers with options to ski shorter distances.

There are some important differences with running. First, if you are a runner with an adequate endurance base, you can safely ski a ski marathon on a limited training schedule. No 65 mile weeks, no 20 mile runs are needed; you can race off what might be considered a 10K base if you pace yourself. I know, because my first ski marathon was only my second ski race ever, and I finished comfortably in the middle of the pack, tired but not wiped out like after a road marathon.

The second major difference is that if you don't go out too fast, there's no "wall" to hit. This comes as a surprise since we know what happens to most runners about 18-20 miles into a marathon, and we tend to expect it while skiing. If you ski smart, you'll not only enjoy the race, but end up without the hobbling that characterizes most marathon endings.

Don't be misled, skiing 31 miles as a beginning skier is no trip through the park. It is a reachable goal, even in the first year of skiing. Do not be put off by the distance or your lack of long training runs or skiing outings. Thousands of citizen racers ski marathons each year. Ski 31 miles wisely and you will not only complete the race, you'll be surprised at how good you feel at the end.

PREPARING TO GO THE DISTANCE

It pays to make the decision to enter a marathon early because there are stiff entry fees which increase as race day nears. It is common to have a $15-20 fee several months before the race and then gradually increase the charge until it is $40 or more by the cutoff date. As noted in Chapter 6, you often don't get too much, besides a good race and a finisher's medal or pin, for your fee. Don't expect T-shirts or some of the other paraphernalia of road racing. Costs are high when 20-30 miles of trails need to be maintained.

Nearly all marathons have a shorter race option, usually 25K, which may be a more comfortable for the first long race. Some races allow you to finish whichever distance you feel up to but usually you will have to declare your option beforehand. Silver finishers' medals/pins are given to 25K finishers and gold to those who complete the 50K.

Race day preparation is much like getting ready to run a marathon. Most

Photo by Thomas J. Kelly/Worldwide Nordic Tours

Marathon skiing has all the trappings of marathon running, including a mob scene at the start.

skiers do some carbo loading the night before — many races feature pasta suppers the night before. It is smart to start hydrating well before the race. Eat a pre-race breakfast of easily digested food. You will find that most skiers race on more food than they would consider before a road race. (The energy demands will be higher and it pays to start off well fueled.) Use petroleum jelly in the crotch, underarms, and nipple areas, like in running. Bring a water bottle and drink, even if it is sub-freezing outside.

Arrive at the race early. Give yourself time to finish waxing (unless you are skating) and also to get to the starting line. There may be a bus ride or some skiing to get to the start, so plan ahead. Give yourself extra time to deal with ice cold Fiberglass johns — the wait is even slower due to the layers that each skier must deal with. Most skiers do not do much pre-race stretching but just do a light warm up and use the first 5K of the marathon to loosen up. Save your energy, it will be a long day.

There are several types of starts used in marathons: mass starts are just like those used in running; wave starts begin groups at intervals (and are timed accordingly). Don't be shy about getting too far up to the front. One runner told me, "After having slower skiers trip and tangle with me for the first couple of kilometers, I vowed never to be so diplomatic about starting again. Now I look for people who look about my speed, and make sure I'm up there with them."

If you love crowds and confusion, you'll have fun at a mass start of a marathon. Skis clacking against skis, a few falls, lots of "sorry" or "easy now" are de rigeur as folks sort themselves out. With skating now so prevalent, starts are even more chaotic as skaters and diagonal striders try to avoid each other. It often takes 5K or so to get things in order but the bot-

Waiting for the bus to the starting line.

tlenecks begin again at the first big hill. The spirit of the racers is great — it is a lot like the first few miles in a big running marathon with everyone full of energy. The trick is to hang in there, stay upright, and try to relax and conserve energy, there's a long race ahead.

RACE DAY STRATEGY

One of the strengths that runners bring to marathon skiing is a sense of pace — the ability to listen to the body and race accordingly. "Go out slow and taper off," is the facetious motto of more than one group of runners. For ski marathoning, it is not bad advice. Take the first 5K at a reasonable pace — don't burn energy needlessly trying to do a lot of passing and jockeying for position. The first part of the race, while you are fresh, is a good time to enjoy the day and the racers around you and consciously work on skiing efficiently.

Unlike road marathons, there is little crowd support except at road crossings and feeding stations. There is, however, a lot of mutual support. Skiers chat with one another about the weather, the wax, the course. On most courses the trees and terrain provide continual variety. Just when you have established an effective marathon skate, you round a bend and there's a hill to climb. It is a 31 mile interval workout with work periods and rest periods, challenging and ever-changing.

When you come to a water stop in a ski marathon, don't be surprised to find warm water or other drink. You may well be offered warm ERG, Gatorade, Kool-Aid, cocoa, or perhaps some blueberry concoction. Drink cold water if you can get it — the body absorbs it the fastest, and if you're moving along, you really don't need any warming up. Take water every 5K

Take liquids at every feeding station during the race.

or so saving sugary drinks until late in the race. Top skiers take a drink in each hand and ski down the course, sipping from each. For most of us, stopping briefly will be more efficient and provide the chance for a quick rest.

Aside from not drinking enough fluids, probably the biggest error newcomers make in marathon skiing is not eating. A lot of energy is expended over four to six hours and skiers need to take nourishment. During my first marathon, (with half a race to go) it seemed strange to be stuffing brownies in my mouth and washing them down with hot chocolate, but it paid off. Unlike running, eating during the race doesn't upset your system. And, if you don't, you may run out of steam before the day is over. More than once in post-race hubbub you hear, "I skipped those feeding stations and just plain died at the end." Marathon foods include chocolate chip cookies, oranges, bananas, corn bread, even slices of pie. This is no time to watch the diet.

After 35K or so, it is a case of concentrating and pushing on. This is where it helps if you have run some marathons. Legs and arms tire and many skiers go through a "What am I doing this for?" period. It helps to vary your stride, to marathon skate or double pole for a bit, anything to use different muscle groups. If you've been skating all along, it may help to put on a little kick wax and diagonal stride for a while. This is a time for caution. Be careful on the downhills when you are tired — take them easy and don't follow closely behind another tuckered skier.

If you ski a smart race, not only will you finish but, because of the smoothness of skiing, you will feel surprisingly spry afterwards; a bit stiff but nothing like the aftermath of a road marathon. That is why elite skiers can do a marathon every week and why so many citizens racers ski several

50K races each winter. The "populist" aspect of race series like the Great American Ski Chase and the new Canadian National Loppet series are a result of the ease with which the challenge of a ski marathon can be met.

LEAF GREAT AMERICAN SKI CHASE

There are several dozen ski marathons in the United States. In the mid-West, the Central Marathon Series consists of 10 regional races where skiers can earn pins for participation and completion of races. There are no other regional marathon series.

One of the best things that has happened to citizens' racing in the United States was the formation in 1979 of the Great American Ski Chase. Comprised of the cream of the ski marathon crop, it is truly a series for everyone. Many runners will enter one of the eight GASC races for their first marathon.

Races are held at locations throughout the country and attract not only hordes of citizens' racers but a few dozen elite skiers who "Follow the Chase." For many, it is exciting to ski in a race with a skier like Bill Koch or Dan Simoneau. The slick factory-team racing suits, the lithe bodies of top-ranked athletes, and the hoopla surrounding Olympic-caliber skiers adds an extra dimension to the race.

The race series gained even more popularity in 1986 when a major international confectionery company, Leaf, Inc. became the major sponsor. In addition to the normal array of food, the feeding stations became a veritable smorgasbord of candy goodies. You haven't experienced true citizens' racing until you've stopped at a 35K station, munched a couple of chocolate cookies, washed them down with warm Gator-Aid, and raced off down the track eating a couple of Clark bars.

The centerpiece of the Leaf Great American Ski Chase series is the Whoppers American Birkebeiner. Patterned after the famous Norwegian Birkebeiner, the race began in 1973 with 74 skiers. It now has more than 7,000 participants. Skiers begin in Hayward, Wisconsin and after skiing down Main Street, wind through the hills and forests for 55 kilometers to finish in front of the Telemark Colosseum in Cable, Wisconsin. Over a quarter of the skiers in the "Birkie" are racing it for the first time. It is a perfect race for a runner to enter for the initial ski marathon.

The other GASC races are smaller in size and each has its unique features. Common denominators of each race are the spirited volunteers who pitch in to help and the elite skiers who ski Chase races.

CANADIAN LOPPET SERIES

There are dozens of Canadian ski marathons to choose from. Called loppets, they range from the Gatineau 55 in Ottawa, one of the stops on the Worldloppet series, to events strung from Nova Scotia to the Yukon. The emphasis is on participation.

Many provinces have a loppet series with the events open to everyone and offering several race distances. Such a series is the British Columbia Loppet Series which has a roster of 12 races. Skiers who complete six in a year earn a T-shirt while bronze, silver, and gold pins can be earned in successive years. The Quebec Loppet Cross-Country Circuit, which celebrates its sixth season in 1987, consists of five major races. Manitoba's eight race series and Alberta's schedule of 13 loppets are indicative of the popularity of marathon skiing in Canada.

To top off these active provincial programs, the Canadian National Loppet series, consisting of premier ski events across the country, is being inaugurated for the 1987 ski season.

WORLDLOPPET

If you have ever run a marathon in another country, you will know the attraction the Worldloppet has for skiers. The chance to compete in a foreign land, whether you are a top-ranked masters or a "back-of-the-packer," is an unforgetable experience.

Just as runners plan vacations around the London or Paris marathons, so do skiers take winter weeks off to experience the original Norwegian "Birkie" or one of the many other international races.

The Worldloppet is a series of eleven races held across the world each year. Top ranked long distance skiers in the world compete in these events yet, like the Leaf Great American Ski Chase, the events are aimed at the average citizen skier. And they show up in droves — over 14,000 ski the Finlandia Hiihto and more than 80,000 skiers took part in the 1986 Worldloppet series.

While the elite skiers race for the series championships, citizen racers can work toward earning a Worldloppet medallion. You have to finish 10 of the 11 races, but, you have a lifetime to do it.

The most famous race of the Worldloppet is the Norwegian Birkebeiner, which has been held since 1932. It commemorates the rescue of the child prince Haakon Haakonss0n by soldiers during a civil war in 1206. The soldiers wore birch leggings and were thus nicknamed "birkebeiners." The race is run between the towns of Lillehammer and Rena in the mountains of

A mass start at a Worldloppet event is something one does not forget.

central Norway. Skiers wear a pack to simulate the weight of the prince. There are two Worldloppet races in North America, the Whoppers American Birkebeiner and the Gatineau 55 in Ottawa. The complete series is described in the Appendix.

A number of tours go to Worldloppet events: WorldWide Nordic USA leads skiers on citizens' race tours across the globe as has Reliable Racing Supply. Get on their mailing list — to ski a foreign marathon is a nice long range objective.

Whether you travel across the globe to ski or sign up for a local loppet, going 31 miles on skis is well within the capability of most runners. The trick is to set an easy pace, take plenty of liquids and food along the way, and enjoy the experience. Don't bother "racing", that can come in later marathons. You will be pleasantly surprised at how great you feel as you cross the finish line, and how spry you are the next morning.

10. Waxing basics for runners

Ever been at big 10K or marathon and been amazed at some of the warm-up routines you see? There might be runners performing stretches that defy description, others chanting or aerobic dancing, still one or two others in some yoga position. For beginning road racers, it can be a shock — I remember thinking, "All I know is about three different stretches. What else can I do?" After a while, we chalk it up to just part of the pre-race "hype" — to each, his or her own.

Waxing, whether for ski racing or just a tour, can take on some of the same elements of trendiness. Skiers, like runners, are not above a little "one-upsmanship" and it is easy to make cross country waxing appear to be an advanced course in organic chemistry. First you look at a wax kit that looks well-supplied enough to equip most ski shops, then you hear, "Well, I found that a soft blue over a special red was just right — I knew the tracks hadn't glazed yet." It's enough to drive you right straight to the no-wax ski sale. But, forget the mystique, waxing can be easily learned and mastered. Even if you've already bought no-wax skis, read on. You can jazz up the performance of your skis by knowing some of the rudiments of waxing. Here are some waxing basics.

First, there are two basic categories of waxes — glide waxes (for the tips and tail surfaces) and for traditional skiing, grip wax (for the center third of the ski base). Grip wax is also known as kick wax. You'll be hearing more and more about ski base preparation and glider wax as you get into cross country skiing, that's where the changes are taking place. All runners who get into skiing should know how to apply glide wax, so we'll cover that first. But before we start dripping molten wax on the carpet, let's find a place to do our waxing.

You need a level surface, preferable waist-high or so, to iron on ski wax. Work benches are fine, although you can use shed or basement floors as well. Find some wooden blocks to rest the skis on — I've nailed a couple of 2 X 6 planks to the workbench. A tailboard that the ski tails rest against is essential, this allows you to scrape the skis against a restrainer. Just temporarily nail a board to the end of the bench. You can use a vise but remember, the sidewalls of skis are fragile. So, with a work area where we can spill wax drippings and scrapings, we have all we need to get going.

At the risk of making waxing appear complicated, let's look at a basic equipment list that a runner should have to get into waxing. (Remember, you can borrow some of this gear — don't rush out and buy $50 worth of materials.)

Liquid Wax Remover — available in most ski shops

Fiberglass scraper

Rags — You can use special lint-free material like Fiberlene

Waxing Iron — An electric iron is most reliable. I bought one for $1.50 that works fine at a Salvation Army outlet. You can also use a propane torch and metal waxing iron.

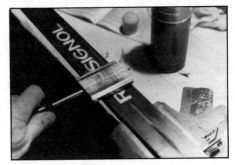

This type of waxing iron is usually heated with a torch.

Fibertex or Scotch Brite Pad

Glide Wax — Universal Glider or violet will work for a most situations

Stiff Plastic Brush — optional

Grip Waxes and Cork

You will see, once you start putting a wax kit together, that the $5.00 wax remover and $2.95 wax tins add up fast. Buy only what you need, and borrow the rest.

GLIDE WAXING

Whether you plan to use no-wax skis, use grip wax for diagonal stride, or skate on skis, you'll want to learn how to prepare and wax the gliding surfaces of your skis. This will be the tips and tails for most skiing, and the whole ski base for ski skating. Glide wax will not only improve the gliding performance of your skis, it also will help protect the bottoms.

In the days of wooden skis, pine tar was used to seal the pores of the base. This smelly, smoky process, utilizing torches, gunky rags, and gooey pine tar, was a satisfying part of the ski preparation ritual for many, and still is for some. Since the advent of fiberglass skis, glider wax has taken the place of pine tar.

Not long ago, skiers simply put a hard grip wax over the pine-tarred bases of their skis, corked it in, and were ready to go. Then, nordic racers, learning from their Alpine teammates, learned how to iron hard wax on to their new fiberglass skis. But alpine racing wax is designed for short fast dashes down the slope and couldn't hold up for the longer cross country races. So a whole new generation of nordic glider waxes was developed. At first, there were only a few gliders; now there is a rainbow of glide wax colors that can befuddle the novice. Glide waxing technique has taken on some of the "mystique" once reserved for grip waxing. Don't get too fancy. Stick with universal glider or violet — either of them will fit the bill for most skiing.

Fiberglass skis have bases made of polyethylene or similar material, commonly called P-Tex. Although it looks smooth to the eye, the surface has thousands of microscopic pores. First, you need to clean the base to get any dirt or old wax off and then fill those pores with a melted glide wax.

If the ski has been previously waxed, remove as much wax as you can with a plastic/fiberglass scraper. Then, clean the base with a wax remover solvent using a rag or a lint-free material like Fiberlene. Let the solvent soak in and then remove it with the rag, wiping off any old wax or dirt. Be cautious with solvent on waxless skis, especially those with a chemical or hairy base. Ask your ski shop for advice. Solvents are volatile, so keep them off your skin and work in a ventilated space. Once the skis are dry, you can get ready to glide wax.

One of the more recent developments in glide waxing is the whole concept of "structuring" the base. Glass-smooth bases, except perhaps in the most frigid conditions, are never as fast as those surfaces with some texture, some grooves. The warmer and wetter the snow, the more the need for grooves to break up the suction between the thin layer of water that the ski glides on and the ski surface. You'll see racers go after their bases with brass brushes in wet conditions or use a special rilling tool to create fine ridges in the ski bases. Rather than get too fancy, we can just buff the tips and tails of no-wax skis (and the whole base on waxables) with a Fibertex or Scotch Brite pad. Wrap the pad around a cork and buff from the tip of the ski toward the tail. It's a little like scrubbing with a face cloth, it not only removes grime from shipping and storage but also opens up the pores. It also helps structure the base by putting tiny longitudinal grooves in the base so the ski will glide better.

Glide waxes are color-coded to match snow conditions. Many ski racers and coaches iron on one glider, often purple, and ski on it until conditions change dramatically. Glide wax is much less temperature critical than the grip waxes.

As noted before, glider wax is applied to the tips and tails on no-wax and grip-waxed skis. The center area, or grip zone, is left as-is. Grip wax will go on there later on. If you are "going naked," that is, ski skating with just glide wax, the whole length of the base is glide-waxed.

Glider is melted on with an iron. The best bet is to use an electric iron — you can keep the temperature under control. Waxing irons that you heat with a torch are fine for the "boonies" where there's no electricity, but they are hard to keep at a regulated temperature. Whatever you use, watch the heat — bases can be ruined by too much heat, you can glaze the surface pores with too hot a temperature. What's right? First, use a temperature that will melt the wax but not make it smoke. Err on the side of coolness. Try the "wool" setting on an electric iron but don't trust the control. Never, in spite of what you may see done by elite skiers, use a torch directly on fiberglass skis. Top skiers have years of experience (plus some company is probably providing skis for them).

Drip dots of glide wax on both sides of the groove in the glide zones, covering about half the surface with wax globs. Run the iron back and forth, working a section at a time, to spread the wax and drive it into the

Melting glide wax on with an electric iron.

pores of the surface. Keep the iron moving, it should be gliding on a molten layer of wax. Watch the heat, pull the iron away if the underside of the ski starts feeling too warm. Many modern skis have foam in them and, being a good insulator, foam can let the heat build up in the base surface fast. Don't worry about wax filling the groove, that will be scraped out later.

You want the ski to absorb the glide wax so keep at it, being wary of the temperature. Check under the extreme tip or tail, the very thin section — it should be warm but not hot. Add wax as it is absorbed. Some coaches recommend that the wax be left for two to three minutes in a molten state on the ski, before you move on to melt in the next section. When the skis have been waxed, set them aside to cool for a half hour or so. Then you will get to remove most of the wax you have just melted on.

Once the skis have cooled, scrape all but a thin layer of the glider wax off the bases. Do this with a sharp plexiglass scraper (which can be kept sharp by filing) using a steady pressure from tip to tail. Note that all the ski prep actions — scraping, cleaning, waxing — are done from tip to tail, to get the surface molecules lined up to head the right way. Draw the scraper down the ski until most of the wax is gone. Don't worry about taking off too much, most skiers leave too much on until they get the hang of it. The colder the weather, the more aggressive you should be in scraping — you can get by with a little thicker layer in warmer snows. Don't forget the groove, use the edge of the scraper to peel off the glide wax.

Most runners can stop at this point and still be a leg up on those who don't glide wax. Those interested in performance will go a step or two further by taking a stiff nylon brush and brush the wax, again from tip to tail.

The final step is to put the skis out in the cold, let them cool, and then brush again. As the skis get cold, wax is squeezed out of the pores and should be removed. This is especially important in very cold conditions.

An application of glide wax will usually be good for days of skiing. If the tracks are icy and harsh, the wax will wear faster. You will note a faint whiteness or white streaks on the bases (on the inner edges if you skate) when it is time to get out the iron again.

If you are dead set against waxing, there are still several products that you can consider to increase your glide speed. Commonly-used products include Maxiglide, Swix Universal Glide Spray, and Toko Touring Glide Wax. These are either sprayed or wiped on the glide surfaces and are good for about a day of skiing.

Runners may choose to forego glide waxing, figuring that their skis are fast enough already. But glide waxing is easy to learn and has to be done only a few times a season in most conditions. It gives you a chance to check over your skis, to "personalize them" for your use. For many skiers, this tinkering with the ski bottoms is an integral part of the preparation for skiing, ranking right behind getting in shape. It is like tuning and cleaning up the bike or working on soles of your running shoes — some runners will like to do it, others will not. But the first time that you are passed on a shallow downhill by someone with comparable gear, you'll think again about glide waxing. We work too hard going up the hills not to get the most out of going down them.

GRIP WAXING

Grip wax, the wax under your foot, provides the "get up and go" for the diagonal stride and other traditional techniques. Waxes come in colors keyed to the snow conditions and temperature. When your skis are waxed properly, each kick and glide moves you effortlessly down the track and all is right with the world. On the other hand, if you slip when you push (wax too hard for snow conditions) or have the glide of a trowel over wet concrete (wax too soft for snow), you're experiencing the darker side of grip waxing, the side of which all the horror stories are made. By knowing the basics, you can learn to wax for any condition. Then, unlike your friend on no-wax skis, you can adapt to meet changing conditions and not have to settle for a compromise in performance.

The type of snow determines which kick wax should be used. Remember the pictures by "Snowflake Bentley," how each snow crystal had an array of spiky points? These sharp spikes penetrate ski wax easily, so we can use a hard wax (like a green) for crisp fresh snow conditions. Once snow warms a bit or has been on the ground for a while, the edges of the flakes become rounded and we need a softer wax, such as a blue. Snow that is good for snowballs requires even stickier wax, like a violet or a red. And when the snow has melted and refrozen, the crusty icy surfaces call for the "Shoe-Goo" of skiing, klister wax. So, although wax selection can seem like an alchemist's fantasy, it comes down to this: the grip wax has to be soft enough to let the snow crystals penetrate when you put your full weight on the ski for the pushoff, yet it must be hard enough to allow the ski to glide cleanly.

Waxing will vary in different parts of the country. Some areas in the West, blessed with uniform powder conditions day after day, make waxing a breeze. Skiers rub on a little Extra Blue and hit the trails again for another outing. ("Special" waxes are slightly harder, for colder snows. "Extra"

Courtesy of Douglas Reid

Rub grip wax on to the center section of the ski.

waxes are softer, e.g. Extra Blue is for slightly warmer snow than Blue.) Skiers in the Pacific Northwest get to know their warm red waxes quite well while many skiers in the Northeast deal with klister for much of the late winter. Talk to your skier friends, see what tins of wax are almost used up — it will give you a good idea of what you might start out with for your basic kit. Don't be shy about borrowing a little wax from them; after all, it takes about a dime's worth of kick wax for a pair of skis.

You can keep grip waxing simple by going to a "two-wax" system. One wax is used for dry snow, colder than freezing, and the other for wet snow. The systems work pretty well, and if you add a tube of universal klister, you can meet all your waxing needs. These systems may be the best bet for many runners who decide to buy waxable skis. Other skiers will want to be more specific in their grip waxing, matching color-coded waxes with the snow conditions. Start off with a wax kit which contains a green, a blue, and a red wax. (Remember, the warmer the color, the warmer the wax.) Each wax has a temperature range shown on it and wax charts can be found in most ski shops. Most skiers use a small thermometer to determine snow and air temperature.

Skis are easiest to grip wax when they are warm and dry. In the real world of skiing, it's not always that way. You'll be standing up against a car, shivering, hustling to rub on wax, hoping that you do it right the first time. Do dry the skis off, wax will not stick to wet skis. Rub the wax on in even strokes in the middle third of the ski, working from tip toward tail. Keep the wax area forward of the heel plate and apply the wax in a smooth layer. (Use the edge of the wax.) Smooth the wax with a cork and let the skis cool outside. Then, ski for a few minutes and see if you are all set.

If the skis are a little slippery, perhaps just a thicker layer of the same wax will provide the grip. You can also try a longer grip waxed area. Then, if this fails, change to a warmer wax, putting it right on top. Remember, TLC — thicker first, then longer, only then change.

If your skis are sticking, you've learned a hard lesson — err on the cold side rather than the warm side. Scrape the wax off quickly and try a colder wax, and file the lesson away.

There are several other basics to keep in mind:

1. Let your skis cool before you check the wax. It takes a while for the wax to set, and if you try them right after waxing, you may get a false reading.

2. If you are skiing in humid conditions, you'll find that you need a softer wax than you might expect from the temperature reading.

3. Breaking trail and touring through back-country will let you wax a little colder than for the prepared tracks — remember, it all depends on the shape of the snow crystals.

Klister. Most of us have got it on parkas, ski books, and ski racks. Frankly, for most runner/skiers, klister wax is a real pain. It has a bad reputation and unless you are really into waxing, it deserves it. But, there are times when the trails are frozen and crusty and klister will be the only thing to get you there and back using the diagonal stride.

Soft klisters like red and violet go on fairly easily if the tube is warm. Squeeze it on like toothpaste and spread it thinly and evenly with the applicator. Then hope that you've got it right for the temperature — it's a good time to let a friend try it and see what klister works. Universal klister is a good bet for most runners who want to get out skiing because it works in a wide range of temperatures.

So, glide waxing is easy, and kick waxing, once we know the basics, is not overwhelming. Waxing has a certain "bubble, bubble, toil and trouble" reputation which it really doesn't deserve. You can make it as complicated as you want or you can keep it simple. If you read the waxing sections of ski books or magazines, it is easy to get confused by the discussions of layering and waxing combinations. But now that most racers, from citizen racers to World Cuppers, use just a glide wax for most races, some of the mystery is already leaving the waxing scene. It is a perfect time for runners to learn the basics and find out how great a properly-waxed pair of cross country skis can perform.

11. On the road again

Cross country skiing comes to a peak in late February/early March in the Eastern U.S. and later in March in the West and throughout Canada. As the sun gets higher in the sky, runners start itching to shed winter windsuits and go out and run bare-legged. If they've been skiing, they feel ready to go out and "burn up the track." But they're not as ready as they think.

Writer/runner Hal Higdon, asked if there are benefits to cross country skiing wrote, "Yes, if it allows you to rest injured running muscles. No, if you come back too soon in the spring and reinjure yourself."

For some runners, the risks in cross country skiing are not found on icy trails or tree-lined curves, they lie on the sun-dried roads of early spring. As the snowbanks recede there is a tendency to go out and run too much. Coach Paul Daly explains, "Runners tend to go overboard in early spring after they drop skiing. They try to run every day."

A lot depends on how often you have been able to run during the winter. If you've run several times a week, the switch to running is easier. Still you have to fight the tendency to overtrain. The transition back to running in the spring is a time for moderation. Even though you may feel like an aerobic horse from a winter's worth of skiing, your legs need time to adjust to the pounding. This is not the time to get hurt.

Masters runner Dick Kendall explains, "Actually, running is a better conditioner for cross country skiing than skiing is for running. That's why I run about three hours a week during the ski season. I do a few strideouts so I remember what leg speed is all about."

Terry Aldrich, veteran coach of skiing and running at Middlebury College, recommends caution in the spring. "The transition from skiing to running has to be a very, very, very careful one," Aldrich says. "If skiers haven't been running during the winter and go out in the spring, even though their cardiovascular systems are fully developed, their running muscles just aren't there. You can do some real damage as far as overuse injuries. If you jump into it too quickly and try a 60 mile week, you'll be bedridden."

Potential problem areas are shin splints, Achilles soreness, tendonitis, or soreness in the hip area. This is a good time to be extra careful with warm-ups, pre and post running stretches, and to make sure that your training flats are well-cushioned.

Coach Aldrich, himself a 2:40 marathoner and 33:00 10K runner, recommends a very gradual progression. "I try to start easy, I've learned that through experience. Unless you've been running, start with a mile or two, every other day. Increase about 5% a week until you get your legs under you. It takes about a month."

One way to help with the transition is to stay on your skis. Spring is a great time to keep on skiing as you pick up the running mileage. Touring is delightful as the sun gets higher in the sky and the days get longer. Not only is it more comfortable weather-wise, there are fewer skiers. As early flowers bloom in the suburbs, there is often plenty of snow left in the woods for touring.

Run every other day or try two days on and one day off. Keep the intensity low through the first month as you build leg strength. On the off days from running, use non-weight bearing workouts such as biking or swimming for aerobic workouts.

Dick Kendall says that it is not that difficult to return to running. Two ski marathons per winter give him all the aerobic base he needs and then it is just a matter of getting the legs used to lifting the body against gravity — slowly increasing the tempo.

Being careful will pay off. With your aerobic base from skiing and a spring tuneup of the running muscles, by the time running season is in full swing you will be ready. And very likely, before the summer solstice, you will be thinking about beginning to train again for your second season — the season of cross country skiing.

Glossary

Aerobic Skiing "with oxygen" at a pace within the training heart rate.

Aerobic Capacity The ability to supply oxygen to the muscle tissues.

Anaerobic Skiing "without oxygen." Also called oxygen debt.

Anaerobic Threshold A borderline, about 85% of the maximum heart rate.

Bail The metal piece that clamps over a boot to hold it to the ski.

Basket The device attached to the bottom of the ski pole to keep the pole from sinking into the snow.

Biathlon A rapidly growing sport which combines marksmanship and cross country skiing.

Bill Koch Ski League The youth program of the U.S. Ski Association.

Binder wax Also called base wax, it is used to make grip wax wear longer.

Biomechanics Using the science of mechanics to study physiological movements.

Bounding Running, usually uphill, using bounding motions to simulate diagonal stride or skating. A key training method.

Camber The arch built into skis to support the skier's weight while allowing the ski to glide.

Carbon fiber A material used in ski pole shafts and skis.

CCC Cross Country Canada, an arm of the Canadian Ski Association.

Chair dip A dip down between two chairs. Used to strengthen the arm muscles and shoulder girdle.

Christie A skidding turn on both uphill ski edges.

Citizens' race A ski race for everyone. Called a *loppet* in Canada.

Cork A block of cork (often synthetic) that is used to polish grip wax.

Delamination   The splitting of fiberglass skis, often at the tails.

Diagonal Stride   The classic cross country technique, similar to running, where the arm and opposite leg swing forward together.

Double camber   The center section of skis where the camber is stiffer.

Double pole   Propelling oneself forward with both poles. An important technique for any skier, not just racers.

F.I.S.   Federation International de Ski, the international governing body for skiing.

Fall line   Shortest line up or down the hill.

Fannypack   A beltlike pack, also called a bumbag.

Fartlek   A training method familiar to runners. Means "speed play" and involves changing speeds during a workout.

Fast-twitch fibers   Muscle fibers that release glycogen rapidly. Skiers/runners with good speed have a high percentage.

Feed   A drink containing sugar and salts such as ERG.

Flat ski   Skiing with the surface flat on the snow. Important in skating.

Flex   How easily a ski or ski pole bends.

Gaiters   Waterproof cuffs used to keep snow out of ski boots.

Glider wax   A hard wax used on the glide zone for diagonal stride and on the whole ski base for skating.

Glycogen   The substance stored in muscles and used up in long races.

Grip   The thrust onto the snow that propels a skier forward in the diagonal stride. Also called kick.

Hard wax   Solid grip wax, such as green, used for new snow.

Heart monitor   A training device strapped across the chest which determines heart rate. Usually has a wristwatch display.

Heel plate   A plate or disk with ridges to keep ski boot heel in place when weight is on the ski.

Herringbone   A "V-walking" movement used to climb steep hills.

Hypothermia   A decrease in body temperature caused by exposure. A potentially serious problem for skiers and runners.

Imagery   A "psyching" technique used to get ready to compete.

Jackrabbit Ski League   Canada's ski program for youth.

Kick See *Grip*.

Kick Turn A method of reversing direction when standing still.

Kicker A grip wax applied in the *wax pocket* of the ski.

Kinesthetic sense Awareness of what is happening to the body.

Klister A sticky liquid wax used when there is refrozen snow.

Knickers Knee length ski pants, used with long socks.

Lactic acid The substance generated at a rate faster than the body can assimilate when skiers/runners go into *oxygen debt*.

Layering Dressing for skiing in layers, usually three. (Wicking, insulation, protection.)

Loppet A "people's race." Called a *citizens' race* in the U.S.

Marathon skate A skating motion used with prepared tracks.

Masters Skiers who are over age 30.

Max oxygen uptake A measure of the capacity of the oxygen system.

Mohair A hairy material used in strips to provide grip on some no-wax skis.

Negative base A patterned waxless base cut into the ski.

Nordic combined An event combining ski jumping and cross country racing.

Nordic norm The standard system used for the 75mm boot/binding system.

No-wax skis Skis that get their grip from a patterned bottom, chemical base, or some other non-wax system.

Offset skating Also called staggered poling, it has become the primary skating technique. Poles are planted sequentially.

One-skate A skating method for the flats and gradual uphills. Double poling thrust on each skate. Requires good balance.

Orienteering Navigation with map and compass to preselected points.

Overboots Light covers that pull over ski boots. Used in cold or wet conditions, especially over thin racing boots.

Oxygen debt Going past the anaerobic threshold in exertion.

P-tex A polyethylene base material, variations of which are used on ski bases.

P-tex candle A stick of plastic which is melted to

repair scratches and gouges on ski bases.

Paper test A method of evaluating camber/stiffness of skis in relation to a skier's weight and ability.

Pine tar A black gooey substance that is used to prepare the base of wooden skis.

Plyometrics Lengthening a muscle (stretching it) before it contracts. The basis of some current skating training methods.

Positive Base A patterned base where the grip surface protrudes from the base.

Pulk A sled pulled by a skier to move kids or provisions.

Pulley A simple way to strengthen arms for poling. Most have variable resistance.

Rilling Cutting fine ridges in the base of the ski to reduce the suction of wet snow. Done with a file or a special tool.

Roller skis Short wheeled skis used to practice in off-season.

Rollerboard A "do-it-yourself" training device for building upper body strength.

Shovel The part of the ski tip that turns upward.

Sidecut The reduction in ski width in the midsection that aids turning.

Sideslip Sliding downhill sideways with control.

Siitonen technique Another name for marathon skating, after Pauli Siitonen, the inventor of the technique.

Skate turn A turn where the skier skates off a weighted ski.

Ski striding Running or walking, often with ski poles.

Skins Long mohair strips that are stuck or strapped to skis to climb. Used primarily in mountaineering skiing.

Slideboard A training system used by speed skaters as well as some skiers. Often a formica counter-top with padded sidewalls.

Slow-twitch fibers Muscle fibers which utilize glycogen efficiently during long duration exercise.

Snowplow Also called *wedge*. A slowing-down maneuver with tips together and ski tails spread apart.

Specificity Training aimed at developing skills and muscles for a particular sport.

Step turn A turn where the ski tips are picked up and moved, one at a time, in a new direction.

Stroke volume The volume of blood pumped by a ventricle of the heart per beat.

Telemark A skiing method featuring turns with flexed knees and the outside ski ahead of the inside ski.

Training effect The exercise level needed to derive benefits, usually 60 to 70% of maximum heart rate.

Training skates A popular type of dryland skating equipment. Plastic molded hockey skates with 3 to 5 two-inch wheels.

Transition snow Snow at the freeze/thaw temperature zone.

Traverse To ski across the hill at an angle to the fall line.

Triathlon A winter event combining running, skiing, and biking. Sometimes ice skating or other events are substituted.

Tuck A crouching downhill position used to cut wind resistance.

Two-wax system A simplified grip wax system with one wax for dry snow and one wax for wet snow.

USSA United States Ski Association

V-skate The skating herringbone that forms the basis of most skating methods.

Wax pocket The section of the ski base marked for grip wax.

Wedge See *Snowplow*

Wind chill Equivalent temperature when wind velocity is considered.

Where to get more information

BOOKS

Caldwell, John. *The Cross-Country Ski Book*. Brattleboro, VT: Stephen Green Press, 1985.

Now in its seventh edition, this is a good basic manual for all aspects of cross country skiing. Good section on waxing.

Caldwell, John and Brady, Michael. *Citizen Racing*. Seattle, WA: The Mountaineers, 1982.

A complete look at racing from two good writers. Excellent photographs of technique.

Cross Country Canada. *The National Guide to Loppet Skiing*. Prepared by Anton Scheier. Canada, 1985.

A technical guide written by Canadian experts on all aspects of loppet/citizens' racing. Excellent drawings of skating techniques.

Hall, Marty. *One Stride Ahead*. Tulsa, OK: Winchester Press, 1981.

A good technical book for runners interested in racing. Hall, former U.S. and current Canadian ski team coach, covers all aspects of ski prep, waxing, training, and racing.

Woodward, Bob. *Cross-Country Ski Conditioning*. Chicago, IL: Contemporary Books, 1981.

Although slightly outdated, this is a practical look at training for skiing. Good section on roller board construction. Aimed at citizen racers.

PERIODICALS

Cross Country Skier. Emmaus, PA.: Rodale Press, Inc.

A glossy look at what is happening in equipment, techniques, and places to ski. Published five times a year.

North Country Skier. Sault Ste. Marie, Ontario.

A Canadian ski journal published in tabloid form four times a year. Excellent technique articles. A good buy for runners/skiers in U.S. or Canada.

NATIONAL SKI ORGANIZATIONS

Due to the transitory nature of many local ski clubs, often the best source of information on what is happening in a given area can come from the regional office of the U.S. Ski Association or Cross Country Canada. Here are the contacts.

UNITED STATES SKI ASSOCIATION
Regional Offices

Eastern Office

Box 727
Brattleboro, Vermont 05301
(802) 254-6077

Central Office

15 Spinning Wheel Road, #422
Hinsdale, IL 60521
(312) 325-7780

Western Office

U.S. Olympic Complex
1750 E. Boulder Street
Colorado Springs, CO 80909
(303) 578-4600

CROSS COUNTRY CANADA
Division Offices

Alberta

14904 - 121A Avenue
Edmonton, Alberta T5V 1A3
(403) 452-4501

British Columbia

1200 Hornby Street
Vancouver, B.C. V6Z 2E2
(604) 687-3333 ext. 54,55

Federation Quebecoise de Ski

4545, av. Pierre-de-Coubertin
C.P. 1000, Succursale M
Montreal, Quebec H1V 3R2
(514) 252-3000 ext 3565

Laurentian Ski Zone

1822A Sherbrooke Street West
Montreal, Quebec H3H 1E4
(514) 374-4700

Manitoba

1700 Ellice Avenue
Winnipeg, Manitoba R3H 0B1
(204) 786-5641

Northern Ontario

176 Old Garden River Road
Sault Ste. Marie, Ontario P6B 5A6
(705) 253-6407

Saskatchewan

1870 Lorne Street
Regina, Saskatchewan S4P 2L7
(306) 522-3651

Nova Scotia

Box 3010 South
Halifax, N.S. B3J 3G6
(902) 425-5450

Southern Ontario

Box 7400, Station B
Willowdale, Ontario M2K 2R6
(416) 495-4210

For other divisions, contact Cross Country Canada
333 River Road
Ottawa, Ontario KIL 8H9
(613) 748-5662

Index

Appendix

MARATHON RACE SERIES
(typical schedules)

WORLDLOPPET

Dolomitenlauf	60K	Austria
Marcialonga	70K	Italy
Konig Ludwig Lauf	65K	Germany
Sapporo Ski Marathon	42K	Japan
Transjurassienne	76K	France
Gatineau 55	55K	Canada
Whoppers American Birkebeiner	55K	United States
Finlandia Hiihto	75K	Finland
Vasaloppet	89K	Sweden
Engadin Skimarathon	42K	Switzerland
Birkebeiner Rennet	55K	Norway

LEAF GREAT AMERICAN SKI CHASE

Jolly Rancher Snow Mountain Stampede	50K	Colorado
Good & Plenty Waterville Valley	50K	New Hampshire
Good & Plenty Tug Hill Tourathon	50K	New York

Whoppers North American Vasa	50K	Michigan
Whoppers American Birkebeiner	55K	Wisconsin
Switzer Minnesota-Finlandia	60K	Minnesota
Jolly Rancher Yellowstone Rendezvous	50K	Montana
Jolly Rancher California Gold Rush	50K	California

CANADIAN LOPPET SERIES

Larch Hills Loppet	40K	British Columbia
Cariboo Marathon	50K	British Columbia
Loppet Montebello	50K	Quebec
Kawartha Tour	50K	Ontario
Canadian Birkebeiner	50K	Alberta
Grand Beach Classic	40K	Manitoba
Gatineau 55	55K	Quebec
Les Adventuriers Marathon	40K	New Brunswick
Sask 60	60K	Saskatchewan
Sibley Tour	50K	Ontario
Loppet Mont Sainte Anne	65K	Quebec

Dick Mansfield is a runner and skier who writes on a number of fitness, aviation, and environmental topics. This is his second book.

Book design and illustrations by Bill Woodruff